Sufism
A Beginner's Guide

ONEWORLD BEGINNER'S GUIDES combine an original, inventive, and engaging approach with expert analysis on subjects ranging from art and history to religion and politics, and everything in-between. Innovative and affordable, books in the series are perfect for anyone curious about the way the world works and the big ideas of our time.

Sufism
A Beginner's Guide

William C. Chittick

A Oneworld Book

First published by Oneworld Publications as
Sufism: A Short Introduction, 2000
Reprinted 2001, 2003, 2005
First published in the *Beginners Guide* series, 2008
Reprinted 2011, 2013, 2019

ISBN 978–1–85168–547–9
eISBN 978–1–78074–052–2

Typeset by Jayvee, Trivandrum, India
Cover design by Two Associates
Printed and bound in Great Britain by Clays Ltd, Elcograf S.p.A.

Oneworld Publications
10 Bloomsbury Street
London WC1B 3SR
England

Stay up to date with the latest books,
special offers, and exclusive content from
Oneworld with our newsletter

Sign up on our website
www.oneworld-publications.com

MIX
Paper from
responsible sources
FSC® C018072

Contents

Contents

Preface

I first began studying Sufism more than thirty years ago as an undergraduate. At that time, few people had ever heard the name, and I constantly had to explain what it was (or what I thought it was at the time). Nowadays, everyone seems to have heard of Sufism, and the name is mentioned in daily newspapers, best-selling novels, and popular movies. Back then Rumi was hardly known outside university courses on Middle Eastern Studies, but today his poetry is found in any bookstore and recited on television by celebrities. The "whirling dervishes" were a piece of exotica left over from nineteenth-century travelers' accounts, but today people learn "Sufi dancing" in health clubs and New Age centers. All this new-found fame might lead us to conclude that Sufism is much better known than it was thirty years ago, but this is not really the case, though a once strange name has indeed become a bit more familiar.

The great surge in books on Sufism over the past few years has made a large amount of information available, but in certain ways it has added to the confusion. The academic books are too specialized and technical to be useful for beginners, and the much greater number of books written by enthusiasts or Sufi teachers present radically different views about Sufism's reality. The scholars impose their own conceptual schemes from the outside, and the enthusiasts look at the tradition from the privileged standpoint of insiders, but limited to specific contemporary branches of Sufism. In this book I have tried to find a middle way between academic obscurity and enthusiast advocacy.

The Sufi tradition is far too vast and diverse to attempt anything like a definitive statement about what it entails, but few would deny that there are unifying themes. In attempting to provide a fair survey of the tradition, I have steered a middle course between generalities and specifics. In each chapter I look at Sufism in respect of a theme, and in each I try to show how basic teachings appear in various guises in diverse circumstances.[1] I have provided a relatively large amount of translation from primary texts, because any attempt to understand Sufism in its own context demands looking at its own ways of expressing itself, not simply at interpretations made in contemporary terms.

My goal throughout is to let the tradition speak for itself. Although this task is almost impossible, the attempt may help set this book apart from other introductory works available in English. I take as my mentor here Abd ar-Rahman Jami (d. 1492), who writes as follows in the introduction to his well-known Sufi classic *Lawa'ih*:

> It is hoped that none will see in the midst the one who has embarked on this explication, or sit on the carpet of avoidance and the mat of protest, since the author has no share save the post of translator, and no portion save the trade of speaker.[2]

A note on sources

This book is based on primary sources written in Arabic and Persian. Arabic is a Semitic language, a sister of Hebrew and Aramaic, and the most important language of Islamic civilization. Literary Arabic was fixed in its current form by the appearance of the Koran in the seventh century. The language has a vast Sufi literature, much of it written by authors whose mother tongue was Persian, Turkish, or one of the many other languages spoken by Muslims. As for Persian, it is an Indo-European language like English and Sanskrit. It became established in its present form in the ninth and tenth centuries, largely under the influence of Islamic learning, so it has a heavy overlay of Arabic vocabulary. It rivaled Arabic as the most important language of Islamic civilization wherever it spread, from Turkey to China, but especially in the Indian subcontinent. Sufi authors play a more central role in Persian than they do in Arabic, if only because many of the greatest Persian poets were steeped in Sufi learning. It is sufficient to mention Sana'i, Nizami, Attar, Rumi, Sa'di, and Hafiz – arguably the six greatest poets in one of the world's greatest poetical traditions.

I will be citing the Koran, the Hadith (the corpus of sayings attributed to Muhammad), and many Sufi teachers, from earliest times down to Jami in the fifteenth century. I have not forgotten that the Sufi tradition has continued to flourish into modern times and that other Islamic languages also have much to offer. But limits have to be drawn somewhere, and the Sufis whom I will be quoting represent the classical formulation of teachings that have permanently colored the tradition.

I will do my best not to overwhelm readers with unfamiliar names and strange words. For the same reason I leave out diacritical marks in transliterating Arabic and Persian words. In the repeated citations from the Koran, chapter and verse are simply mentioned in parentheses or brackets. In the midst of passages quoted from Sufi texts, Koranic verses are italicized, which helps avoid excessive use of quotation marks and reproduces something of the feel that the verses have for readers of the original works. All translations are my own.

The Sufi path

More than a thousand years ago, a teacher called Ali the son of Ahmad, who hailed from the town of Bushanj in eastern Persia, complained that few people had any idea of what "Sufism" was all about. "Today," he said, speaking Arabic, "Sufism is a name without a reality, but it used to be a reality without a name."

Nowadays in the West, the name has become better known, but its reality has become far more obscure than it ever was in the Islamic world. The name is a useful label, but the reality will not be found in definitions, descriptions, and books. If we do set out looking for the reality, we will always have to keep in mind that the divide between our own times and the times of Ali ibn Ahmad Bushanji – when the various phenomena that came to be named "Sufism" were just beginning to have a shaping effect on Islamic society – is so deep and stark that it may be impossible to recover anything more than the dimmest trace of it.

One easy way to avoid searching for Sufism's reality is to replace the name with another name. We often hear that Sufism is "mysticism" or "esoterism" or "spirituality," usually with the adjective "Islamic" tacked on front. Such labels can provide an orientation, but they are both far too broad and far too narrow to designate the diverse teachings and phenomena that have been identified with Sufism over history. They can never do more than hint at the reality Bushanji had in mind, and they may be more of a hindrance than a help, because they encourage people to file Sufism away unthinkingly into a convenient category. In order to justify using one of these alternative names, we would have to provide a detailed and careful definition and analysis of the new term, and the three I mentioned are

notoriously vague. Even if we could provide an adequate definition, we would still have to explain why it is appropriate for
"Sufism." That would lead to picking and choosing among Sufi
and scholarly writings to support our own definition. We may
get closer to the reality of our definition, but probably not to the
reality that Bushanji was talking about.

Rather than trying to domesticate Sufism by giving it a more
familiar label, we should recognize at the outset that there is
something in the Sufi tradition that abhors domestication and
definition. It may be helpful to suggest that Sufism has a family
resemblance with other traditions – such as Kabbalah, Christian
mysticism, Yoga, Vedanta, or Zen – but making this connection
does not necessarily help us get any closer to Sufism itself.

If we look at the Arabic original of the word *Sufism* (*sufi*), we
see that the term is already problematic in Islamic civilization.
Although it was widely used in several languages, it usually did
not have the broad meaning that it has now acquired. Its current
high profile owes itself mainly to the writings of Western scholars. As Carl Ernst has pointed out in his excellent introduction
to the study of Sufism, the word was given prominence not by
the Islamic texts, but rather by British Orientalists, who wanted
a term that would refer to various sides of Islamic civilization
that they found attractive and congenial and that would avoid
the negative stereotypes associated with the religion of Islam –
stereotypes that they themselves had often propagated.[1]

In the Islamic texts, there is no agreement as to what the word
sufi means, and authors commonly argued about both its meaning
and its legitimacy. Those who used the word in a positive sense
connected it with a broad range of ideas and concepts having to
do with achieving human perfection by following the model of
the prophet Muhammad. Those who used it in a negative sense
associated it with various distortions of Islamic teachings. Most
Muslim authors who mentioned the word took a more nuanced
stand, neither accepting it wholeheartedly nor condemning it.

The modern studies of Sufism reflect the disagreements over the word found in the primary texts. Scholars do not agree among themselves as to what the name means, and any number of definitions and descriptions can be culled from their studies. I will not add to the confusion by providing my own definition, but I will use the word because it seems less inadequate than the alternatives. My purpose, however, will be to try to get at the reality behind the name, to provide a series of pointers at the moon.

The Islamic context

It is not uncommon to meet people in the West who are familiar with certain Sufi teachings and practices but who are ignorant of, or would deny, anything more than an accidental relationship between Sufism and Islam. There are books that enthusiastically acclaim Sufism as an exalted wellspring of spirituality and beauty, while considering Islam, if it is mentioned at all, in terms of the stereotypes that have haunted the West since the Middle Ages. This commonly encountered view of Sufism has been strengthened by the reaction of many modern-day Muslims against it. The great historian of Islamic civilization, H. A. R. Gibb, pointed out fifty years ago that such Muslims look upon Sufism either as a "survival of superstitions" and "cultural backwardness" or as a deviation from "true Islam." Gibb was sufficiently sensitive to Sufism's reality to perceive that such attitudes seem bent on "eliminating the expression of authentic religious experience" from the Islamic world.[2]

In short, many people, both Muslims and non-Muslims, consider "Sufism" as alien to "Islam," however these two terms are defined. But, from the first appearance of teachers who came to be designated as Sufis in the ninth century (the third Islamic century), they have always claimed to speak for the heart and marrow of the Islamic tradition. My first task here is to try to shed some light on their point of view. What role did they accord Sufism within Islam? This question is not as irrelevant today as some people might think, 'because most of those who now speak for the Sufi tradition – at least within the Islamic world itself – have kept the same understanding.

In the early texts, scores of definitions were offered for the words "Sufi" and "Sufism," just as scores of definitions were offered for numerous other technical terms associated with the same teachers.[3] Although it would be possible to begin with one or more of these definitions, it may be more useful simply to suggest that Gibb is on the right track when he implies that Sufism is equivalent to "authentic religious experience." In other words, the early Sufi teachers held that they spoke for the animating spirit of the Islamic tradition. From their point of view, wherever this spirit flourishes, Islam is alive to its own spiritual and moral ideals, but to the extent that it languishes, Islam becomes desiccated and sterile, if it survives at all. This identification of Sufism with Islam's spirit is prefigured in a famous saying of the Prophet known as the "Hadith of Gabriel." Reflecting on the content of this saying can help us situate Sufism's reality in relation to other realities that were given names over the course of Islamic history.

According to this hadith, the Prophet and a few of his companions were sitting together when a man appeared and asked him several questions. When the man departed, the Prophet told his companions that this had been the angel Gabriel, who had come to teach them their religion (*din*). As outlined by Gabriel's questions and the Prophet's answers, the religion of Islam can be understood to have three basic dimensions. Those familiar with the Koran, the wellspring of Islamic teachings, will recognize these three as constant Koranic themes, though nowhere does the Koran provide such a clear and succinct overview. The three are "submission" (*islam*), "faith" (*iman*), and "doing the beautiful" (*ihsan*).[4]

The Prophet defined submission as "to bear witness that there is no god but God and that Muhammad is His messenger, to perform the daily prayers, to pay the alms tax, to fast during Ramadan, and to go on the pilgrimage to Mecca if you can find the means to do so." He said that faith is "to have faith in God, His angels, His scriptures, His messengers, and the Last Day, and to have faith in the measuring out, both the good of it and the evil of it." He said that doing the beautiful is to "worship God as if you see Him, for even if you do not see Him, He sees you."

The first two categories, "submission" and "faith," are familiar to all students of Islam. They correspond to the religion's "Five Pillars" and its "three principles," or to practice and belief, or to the Sharia (the revealed law) and the creedal teachings. The "Five Pillars" are voicing the testimony of faith, doing the daily prayers, paying the alms tax, fasting during the month of Ramadan, and making the pilgrimage to Mecca. The "three principles" are the assertion of divine unity (*tawhid*), prophecy, and eschatology. What needs to be noticed is that the third category mentioned in the hadith – "doing the beautiful" – is just as important for the Prophet's definition as the other two, but its meaning is not nearly as clear.

"Doing the beautiful" is not discussed by the most vocal of the scholars who speak for Islam, that is, the jurists (*fuquha'*). By self-definition they limit their field of vision to the Sharia, which defines the Five Pillars and the other practices that Muslims need to perform. Nor is doing the beautiful discussed by a second influential group of scholars, the theologians (*mutakallimun*), who are the experts in the science of Kalam, or dogmatic theology. Their concern is to articulate and defend creedal teachings, which establish and explain the meaning of the three principles. Neither of these schools of thought has the interest or the competence – qua jurists and theologians – to deal with doing the beautiful, so we would be wasting our time if we read their books looking for an explanation. It is the Sufis who take doing the beautiful as their own special domain.

In order to understand why the great Sufi teachers considered themselves genuine Muslims deeply involved with everything that God and Muhammad have asked from human beings, we need to grasp the logic of this tripartite division of the Islamic tradition and the special role played by doing the beautiful.

On the most external level, Islam is a religion that tells people what to do and what not to do. Right and wrong practices are delineated and codified by the Sharia, which is a compendium of systematic law based squarely on Koranic teachings and prophetic practice, but adjusted and refined by generations of scholars. The Sharia can be likened to Islam's "body," because it designates proper activities, all of which are performed by the body, and because it supports the tradition's life and awareness.

On a deeper level, Islam is a religion that teaches people how to understand the world and themselves. This second dimension corresponds to the mind. It has traditionally been called "faith," because its points of orientation are the objects to which faith attaches – God, the angels, the scriptures, the prophets, and so on. These are mentioned constantly in the Koran and the Hadith, and investigation of their nature and reality became the domain of various disciplines, such as Kalam, philosophy, and theoretical Sufism. Any serious attempt to investigate these objects globally cannot fail to investigate the deepest questions of human concern. The great philosophers, mathematicians, astronomers, and physicians of Islam, who have been studied and admired by many Western historians, were trained in this dimension of the religion. So also, the most famous of the Sufis were thoroughly grounded in the theoretical knowledge of the objects of faith.

On the deepest level, Islam is a religion that teaches people how to transform themselves so that they may come into harmony with the ground of all being. Neither activity nor understanding, nor both together, are humanly sufficient. Activity and understanding need to be focused in such a way that they bring about human goodness and perfection. This goodness is inherent and intrinsic to the original human disposition (*fitra*), created in God's image. If the first dimension of Islam keeps in view the activities that must be performed because of our relational situation with God and others, and the second our understanding of self and others, the third points the way to achieving nearness to God. For those with any sensitivity to the religious life, the various terms that are employed in discussing the focus of this third dimension are immediately recognizable as the heart of religion. These include sincerity, love, virtue, and perfection.

Three domains of faith

The Hadith of Gabriel talks about *iman* or "faith" in terms of its objects, and these specify points of reference that are needed to understand the nature of things. In another hadith, the Prophet spoke about the meaning of the word *iman* itself. "Faith," he said, "is to acknowledge with the heart, to voice with the tongue, and to act with the limbs."[5] This hadith suggests that human beings are compounded of three domains ranked in a clear hierarchy – heart or inmost awareness, tongue or articulation of understanding, and limbs or bodily parts. These three domains are distinct, yet thoroughly intertwined. Inasmuch as they are distinct, they came to be studied by different disciplines and judged by different standards.

"Acting with the limbs," or putting faith into practice, is the domain of jurisprudence. It is here that people "submit" to God's will by obeying the commands set down in the Sharia.

"Voicing with the tongue" is the realm of expressing faith through articulated self-awareness, or rational speech. Human beings are differentiated from other animals precisely by their power of speech, which expresses and conveys the awareness hidden in the depths of the heart. As a domain of learning, voicing faith belonged to those Muslim scholars who investigated the best ways to understand God, the universe, and the human soul.

Finally, "acknowledging with the heart" is to recognize the truth and reality of faith's objects in the deepest realm of human awareness. The "heart" in Koranic terms is the center of life, consciousness, intelligence, and intentionality. The heart is aware and conscious before the mind articulates thought, just as it is alive before the body acts. Faith's inmost core is found only in the heart. The Prophet seems to be referring to this core when he says, "Faith is a light that God casts into the heart of whomsoever He will."

The Prophet's tripartite definition of faith designates the same three domains as the Hadith of Gabriel – body, tongue, and heart; or activity, thought, and awareness. The body's realm is defined by the Sharia, the tongue's realm is expressed in theology (in its various forms, not simply Kalam), and the heart's realm is associated with doing the beautiful in the depths of the soul. To achieve the last, the heart must be rooted in awareness of truth and reality in a pre-cognitive manner. Beautiful acts must well up from the depths of the heart spontaneously, before mental articulation and physical activity. More will be said about what this implies as we go along. This is only the first finger pointing at the moon.

In short, the Islamic tradition recognizes three basic domains of religiosity – body, tongue, and the depths of the heart. These are the domains of right doing, right thinking, and right seeing. The last is an inner awareness of the reality of things that is inseparable from our mode of being in the world. The three realms can also be called perfection of acts, perfection of understanding, and perfection of self. All three are understood and conceptualized as ideals that must be realized in order to live up to the potentialities that were given to human beings when God created Adam in His own image.

These three domains were intensely scrutinized by serious Muslims – those who came to be known as the Muslim "scholars" (*ulama'*). The domain of right activity was the specialty of jurists, that of right thinking the specialty of theologians, and that of right seeing the specialty of Sufis. "O God," the Sufis like to quote the Prophet as saying, "show us things as they are." One does not see things as they are with the eyes or the mind, but rather with the core of the heart. From the heart, right seeing will then radiate forth and permeate every pore of the body, determining thought and activity.

The Shahadah

In this brief outline of the basics of Islam, it is important to notice the primary place accorded to the dual Shahadah or "testimony of faith." This is to bear witness that "There is no god but God" and that "Muhammad is His messenger." The Shahadah provides the key to understanding the Islamic perspective in all domains.

In the definition of "submission," the Shahadah is listed as the first required act of Muslims. By verbally acknowledging the reality of God and the prophetic role of Muhammad, one makes the other four pillars and the Sharia incumbent upon oneself.

The Shahadah also defines the content of faith, whose primary element is faith in God. The nature of the God in whom Muslims have faith is set down briefly by the first Shahadah, while all the objects of faith are conceptualized in terms of the concomitants of the second Shahadah, which designates the domain of the message and the messenger.

Finally, it is impossible to understand what "doing the beautiful" entails unless we know what human beings are, and this knowledge also wells up from the Shahadah. To know the reality of human beings is to know how God impinges on the human situation, because the human image of God cannot be understood apart from the object that it reflects. Human goodness and perfection can be achieved only in terms of God on the one hand and those who have already achieved it on the other, and these are the prophets, Muhammad in particular. This achievement is to actualize the divine image inherent in the soul, and this depends upon putting the Shahadah into practice.

All three dimensions of Islam have been present wherever there have been Muslims. People cannot take their religion seriously without engaging their bodies, their minds, and their hearts; or their activity, their thinking, and their being. But these dimensions became historically differentiated in many forms, the diversity of which has all sorts of causes, about which historians have written no end of books. After all, we are talking about how Muslims practice their religion, how they conceptualize their faith and their understanding of things, and how they express their quest to be near to God. We are talking about various branches of Islamic law and institutions of government, diverse schools of thought investigating the nature of God and the human soul, and multifarious organizations that guide people on the path of spiritual aspiration and give focus to their vastly different experiences of God's presence.

These diverse expressions of Islam, which have undergone tremendous historical and regional variation, have been given many names over Islamic history. The whole situation has become much more complex because of the investigations of modern scholars, who have had their own programs, agendas, and goals and who have employed diverse interpretative schemes in their attempts to make sense of Islamic history in contemporary terms.

In short, Islam, like any full-blown religion, embraces the whole range of human activities and concerns, and the Islamic approach to these has become manifest in a great variety of forms and institutions over history. In contrast to contemporary stereotypes, Islam has a special affinity for diversity of expression. Part of this has to do with the fact that there is no centralized authority comparable to a priesthood or the Catholic church. Instead, Islamic civilization has produced a variety of institutional forms that have come and gone, and all of them have transmitted and inculcated practice, understanding, and the interior life.

As Islam gradually assumed its specific historical forms through the codification of various teachings and practices and the establishment of social institutions, the three dimensions designated by the Hadith of Gabriel came to be reflected within society as relatively distinct, though thoroughly interrelated, aspects of Islamic civilization. However, doing the beautiful remained an intangible inner sanctum. On the individual level, this third dimension has been found in the heart of all Muslims who practice their religion for God's sake alone. In the social sphere it has been given its clearest expression in the life of those whom I would like to call the "Sufis," even though many who claimed this label for themselves did not live up to the ideal, and many who did in fact live up to it did not want the name.

Sufism in this understanding can be viewed as an invisible spiritual presence that animates all authentic expressions of Islam. The various historical forms in which it has appeared serve to demonstrate that this dimension of the religion has remained an ideal of fundamental importance. Nonetheless, the difficulty of achieving human perfection has meant that the individuals and institutions historically connected with the name cannot necessarily be held up as expressions of Sufism's true nature. The Sufis themselves have always been aware of the danger of degeneration and corruption inherent in attempting to adapt social institutions to ideals that can only be fully actualized by rare individuals. When Bushanji said that Sufism is now a name without a reality, he was referring to these inadequate attempts to codify and institutionalize the heart of the tradition.

Mercy and wrath

Sufi teachers have frequently explained Sufism's role in the context of *tawhid*, the assertion of God's unity that is given its most succinct expression in the first Shahadah, *la ilaha illa Allah* "(There is) no god but God." By creating the universe, God causes multiplicity to appear from unity. He displays the potentialities of existence implied by His own "names and attributes" (*asma' wa sifat*) in an infinite universe. The creatures of this universe make manifest the nature of their Creator. The tremendous diversity of creation discloses the unlimitedness of God's creative power. All opposition and strife express the boundless range of God's perfections and the fact that the richness of the divine reality can only appear outside of itself in a domain of infinite differentiation and dispersion. The contrasting and conflicting things of the world can never achieve the peace and stillness of the divine, which alone is the coincidence of opposites.

Many Sufis reduce the basic archetypes for all plurality and multiplicity to two divine attributes – beauty and majesty, or mercy and wrath, or gentleness and severity. The created traces of mercy and wrath can be pictured in terms of the yin-yang symbol. Just as there is no pure yin or pure yang (as represented by the black dot in the white half and the white dot in the black half), so also there is no pure mercy or pure wrath in the created domain. Wherever mercy displays its signs and traces within creation, there will also be manifestations of wrath, and vice versa. In the world as we experience it, certain things display the attribute of wrath more directly, and others are dominated by mercy. In general, things pertaining to the external and material realms tend to manifest wrath, whereas the closer we move to the spiritual world, the closer we approach pure mercy. As Rumi puts it, "This world is the house of God's severity,"[6] which is to say that the other world is the house of God's gentleness and mercy.

Given that God's wrath is associated with this world's distance from God, it is also closely associated with the Sharia, which concerns itself with the outermost human domain, that of bodily activity. However, the wrath that shows its face in the Sharia derives from God's mercy and leads back to it. Although mercy and wrath have a yin-yang sort of relationship in this world, the two do not have equal weight with God. A famous prophetic saying tells us that God's mercy takes precedence over His wrath, which is to say that God's essential nature is mercy and gentleness, and that wrath and severity pertain to the domain of created things. The rather stern and forbidding face of the Sharia, which demands that people follow its commandments or taste the chastisement of hell, displays God's majesty and severity, but lurking beneath its surface is the promise of the precedent mercy. All things came forth from mercy, and all will return to mercy in the end.

Once we see the parallel between the Sharia and the divine majesty and wrath, it is easy to discern a relationship between the spiritual perfection that is sought by the Sufis and the divine mercy, gentleness, and beauty. Here love, central to the expression of Sufi teachings, also enters the picture. Mercy's connection with love is especially obvious on the level of theology, because both mercy and love are said to be the cause of creation. According to the great Sufi theoretician Ibn Arabi (d. 1240), the divine mercy that gives rise to the universe is existence itself. The very act of bringing things into existence is an act of gentleness and kindness. The same point is made in terms of love in a saying constantly quoted in Sufi texts: "I was a Hidden Treasure," God says, "so I loved to be known. Hence I created the creatures that I might be known."

God's mercy and love give rise to the world, but there is an important difference between the two attributes. Mercy flows in one direction, from God to the world, but love moves in both directions. People can love God, but they cannot have mercy upon Him, only upon other creatures. When Sufis say that God's love for creation gives existence to the universe, they quickly add that the corresponding human love for God closes the gap between God and His creatures. Human love makes itself known in sincerity of devotion to the One God. The greater the love, the greater the degree of participation in the divine image, and the greater the degree of human perfection. Hence "love" is often taken as a synonym for doing the beautiful.

The differing theoretical and practical emphases of Islam's three dimensions help explain why Westerners can be simultaneously attracted by Sufism and repelled by "Islam." Such people typically have no knowledge of Islam except the stereotypes that have been passed down from the Middle Ages, or they identify Islam with the Sharia, or with various political and social movements among contemporary Muslims. To the extent that they are aware of the Sharia and the more external aspects of Islamic life and civilization, they are repelled by the sternness and severity of the divine wrath. In contrast, Sufism – whose characteristic expressions are found in beauty, love, poetry, and music – illustrates the dimension of divine beauty and mercy. When Gibb writes that "the aesthetic element in Sufism plays a part which can hardly be overemphasized in its later expression,"[7] he is pointing to the appreciation of beauty and love that is a hallmark of the Sufi tradition.

When Westerners take their first look at Islam, they often feel as if they have been taken into a desert and set down outside the austere walls of a city that smells of death. In contrast, when they are drawn to Sufism, they enter the delightful gardens that are hidden by the walls surrounding traditional Muslim houses. In a living Islamic community, the walls protect the garden from the desert winds and the eyes of strangers, but the garden and the human warmth inside the walls are the reason for the walls' existence.

Sufi theory

The Sufi view of reality derives from the Koran and the Hadith, but it has been amplified and adapted by generations of Sufi teachers and sages. It provides a map of the cosmos that allows people to understand their situation in respect to God. It explains both what human beings are, and what they should aspire to be. It sets down a practice that can lead people from their actual situation to the final goal of human life, or from imperfection to perfection.

The first Shahadah – "(There is) no god but God" – discerns between the Real and the unreal, or between the Absolute and the relative, or between God and "everything other than God," which is the universe. Traditionally the Shahadah is said to be divided into two halves, the negation ("no god") and the affirmation ("but God"). The first half denies the inherent reality of the world and the self. The second half affirms the ultimacy of the divine reality. The Shahadah means that there is "no creator but God," "none merciful but God," "none knowing but God." In sum, it means that there is "no reality but God" and that all the so-called realities of our experience are secondary and derivative.

Numerous Koranic verses and hadiths reiterate the basic discernment contained in the Shahadah and explain its ramifications. One of the most often cited in Sufi texts is the verse, "Everything is perishing but His face" (28:88). As one of the Sufi masters explains,

> God did not say, "will perish," for He wanted it known that the existence of all things is perishing in His Being *today*. Only those still veiled [from the reality of things] postpone the observance of this until tomorrow.[8]

God's reality is such that nothing can stand up to it. His unique possession of all that is real and all that provides reality to "others" means that the others are in fact nonexistent. This is how the Sufis interpret the saying of the Prophet, "God was, and nothing was with Him." The great Sufi shaykh Junayd (d. 910) added, "And He is now as He was." Only God is, and everything that appears to exist along with Him has no true existence. Ibn Arabi remarked that there was really no need for Junayd to add the clarification, because the verb "was" in reference to the Eternal denotes all tenses. "God was," "God is," and "God will be" all have the same meaning.[9]

The primary discernment between the Real and the unreal, or between God and the world, is followed by a secondary discernment among the realities of the world. The second Shahadah tells us that "Muhammad is the messenger of God." It follows that he is a clear, designated manifestation of the One Real. In other words, he represents God more directly than other creatures. He and the Koran for which he is the vehicle are guiding lights in the darkness of unreal things. More generally, all prophets have been sent to reveal God's guidance and mercy to human beings, so revelation plays a special role in human becoming. Without the revealed guidance, people can only wander in ignorance and illusion, immersed in the unreal things that veil them from the truth.

On closer examination, the distinction between divine revelation and all that does not reveal God is much more subtle than at first appears. The Koran calls its own verses and other divine revelations "signs" (ayat), and it employs the same word to refer to the things of the universe. If the Koran is God's Book, displaying His "signs," so also the universe is God's Book announcing His revelations. It follows that the world and everything within it can be viewed from two points of view. In one respect, all things are "other than God" and hence unreal. In another respect, all things are "signs" of God and therefore real in some degree. Here then we have a further discernment of fundamental importance – between phenomena as "signs" and phenomena as "veils."

Sufis explain the distinction between signs and veils employing many sets of terms. According to one formulation, each
existent thing can be said to have two faces. These two faces are
the "eastern face" and the "western face." If we look at the
western face of things, we find no trace of the sun, since it has
set. If we look at the eastern face of the same things, we see the
sun shining in its full glory. Everything displays both faces at the
same time, but the vast majority of people see only the western
face. They have no awareness that everything is a sign of God in
which He is disclosing His own reality. For them, the Koranic
verse, "Wherever you turn, there is the face of God" (2:115), is
a dead letter. In contrast, the prophets and the great Sufis see the
eastern face. They witness God in everything. In their case. God
has answered the prayer, "Show us things as they are." For
them, all things are truly and actually signs of God.[10]

Islamic anthropology pictures human beings as the only
creatures who have freely chosen God over the world, the Real
over the unreal, the East over the West. In the Koran, this free
choosing of God is called the "Trust." "We offered the Trust to
the heavens and the earth and the mountains, but they refused
to carry it and were afraid of it; and human beings carried it."
But, the verse concludes, they are "very ignorant, great wrong-
doers" (33:72). This suggests that they have failed to live up to
their freely chosen responsibilities.

Many would object that they have never made any such
choice. The Sufis typically respond that the objection is
contradictory. Every time we undertake the slightest volitional
act, we have freely accepted our human condition as a given. To
be human is to possess a degree of freedom, and to make choices
is to put oneself in the position of having to answer for the
choices. Rumi provides many entertaining arguments to show
that attempts to shuck off responsibility are always self-serving.
People try to do so only when they are confronted with a choice
that they do not want to make. Otherwise, every time they see

a course of action that suits their fancy, they freely enter into it, knowing all the while that their choices will have consequences.

> Like a hypocrite, you offer your excuses –
> "I'm so busy providing for wife and children,
> "I don't have time to scratch my head.
> How could I have time to practice religion? . . .
> "I cannot escape from feeding my family,
> I must seek lawful earnings tooth and nail.". . .
> You have an escape from God – but not from food.
> You have an escape from religion – but not from idols.[11]

To carry the Trust people must follow the guidance of those who have already carried it, and such people are known as "prophets." More specifically, to be Muslim and Sufi, one submits to God by acknowledging the truth of the Shahadah, by having faith in God and in the perfectibility of human nature as taught in the Koran, and by living the spiritual virtues that are embodied in Muhammad and the great exemplars of the tradition.

In short, the initial discernment between God and the world leads to two secondary discernments, both expressed at least implicitly in the statement, "Muhammad is the messenger of God." People need to discern between revelation and human knowledge, or between the Koran and merely human attempts to understand. They also need to discern between eastern faces and western faces, or between signs and veils. Once they make the discernments, they need to put them into practice. The religious teachings and institutions provide the practical means to choose eastern faces over western faces.

In questions of discernment, the difference between the general Islamic viewpoint and the specifically Sufi perspective does not lie in principles, but rather in a certain self-conscious application of principles. The Sufis do not consider it sufficient for people to have faith and to submit themselves to the Sharia if they also have the capacity of deepening their understandings, purifying their hearts, and doing what is beautiful. In order to reach human perfection, it is not enough to imitate others and follow religion blindly (*taqlid*). Rather, one must achieve a total awareness of the principles and the spirit that animate the religion, or, as the Sufis express it, one must realize the Real Itself (*tahaqquq*). On the theoretical level, the Shahadah becomes a concrete expression of the absolute reality of God, a sword that cuts away the illusory from the Real. On the practical level, the guidelines set down by the Sharia perform the same function, but here Sufis do not accept these guidelines "because they must," but because of their awareness that these play a basic role in allowing human beings to act in accordance with revealed truth and avoid error.

Sufi practice

If Sufism is an appropriate name for doing what is beautiful and striving after spiritual perfection, then it is built on two founda-tions – *islam* or submission to God (the practice of the Sharia and the prophetic model) and *iman* or faith (acceptance of basic Islamic teachings concerning God, prophecy, and the Last Day). Once seekers have gained sufficient grounding in these two dimensions, they can focus their efforts on "worshiping God as if they see Him." Eventually, sincerity and love may take them to the place where the "as if" ceases to apply. In other words, they will worship Him while seeing Him. An often cited model here is the Prophet's cousin and son-in-law Ali, who said, "I would not worship a Lord whom I do not see."

Like Sufi faith, Sufi practice is rooted in the Shahadah. Hence it combines two complementary perspectives – negation and affirmation, or "no god" and "but God." The "god" or false reality that needs to be negated is the individual self or ego, the face turned toward the west and oblivious of the east. As long as self-awareness is dominated by the ego, people will not be able to see the sun's light. Instead, they will perceive a multitude of shadows, false realities, and "idols." In Rumi's words, "The mother of all idols is your own ego."[12]

The actual path of Sufism entails a process of inner transformation whereby the powers of the soul are turned toward God. Sufism adds to the strictly Shariite practices many devotional and spiritual exercises. The most important of these, around which the others are ranged as so many auxiliary means, is the "remembrance" (dhikr) of God, which the Koran commands people to perform in many verses. Remembrance was taught by the Prophet to his close companions in the specific forms that make up the kernel of Sufi discipline.

The "normal" human situation is one of forgetfulness and heedlessness. The least precondition for human perfection is to recognize one's own imperfection and to remember the perfection of the one Reality. But in order to remember the Real in Its fullness, seekers must forget the unreal, which is the western face of their own selves and the world.

In the Koran and in Islamic usage in general, the command to "remember" God also means to "mention" God, so the actual means of remembering God is the mention of God's name (or names). The name is considered to be the direct manifestation of the divine on the human level. Through a gradual process of transformation, the name fills up the mind and consciousness, leaving no room for remembrance of others. The basic insight here is that awareness is the fundamental reality of human nature, and its content determines who we are. As Rumi puts it,

> You are your thought, brother,
>> the rest of you is bones and fiber.
> If you think of roses, you are a rosegarden,
>> if you think of thorns, you're fuel for the furnace.[13]

Constant focus on God leads eventually, God willing, to the goal of the Sufi path, which is "union" with God, or the full realization of human perfection, or actualization of the divine image in which human beings were created. Once perfection is achieved, the separation between the divine and the human that was envisaged in the original discernment has been overcome, at least from a certain point of view. The west has disappeared because the Sun has risen.

Having traversed the path, the Sufis can say with Hallaj (d. 922), "I am the Real," that is, "I am God." This will be no baseless claim, for they will simply be seeing the reality of their own situation. Or rather, these words will be nothing but the Sun showing its rays. This is the final realization of the initial discernment, the fact that "God is, and nothing is with Him." Illusory selfhood has been negated and God alone has been affirmed. "No god" has taken away all impermanent things, and "but God" has left that which truly is. As Rumi puts it,

When Hallaj's love for God reached its utmost limit, he became his own enemy and he naughted himself. He said, "I am the Real," that is, "I have been annihilated; the Real remains, nothing else." This is extreme humility and the utmost limit of servanthood. It means, "He alone *is*." To make a false claim and to be proud is to say, "You are God and I am the servant." In this way you are affirming your own existence, and duality is the necessary result. If you say, "He is the Real," that too is duality, for there cannot be a "He" without an "I." Hence the Real said, "I am the Real." Other than He, nothing else existed. Hallaj had been annihilated, so those were the words of the Real.[14]

2
The Sufi tradition

In a broad sense, Sufism can be described as the interiorization and intensification of Islamic faith and practice. The Arabic word *sufi*, however, has been used in a wide variety of meanings over the centuries, both by proponents and opponents, and this is reflected in both the primary and secondary sources.

The derivation of the word has often been debated. Modern scholars have concluded that the most likely original meaning was "one who wears wool." It is said that by the eighth century (the second century of Islam) the term was sometimes applied to people whose ascetic inclinations led them to wear coarse and uncomfortable woolen garments. Gradually it came to designate a group who differentiated themselves from other Muslims by stressing certain specific teachings and practices of the Koran and the Prophet.

By the ninth century, a great variety of approaches to Islamic learning had developed. The proponents of each discipline considered it essential for understanding the Koran and the Hadith. At this time some of those who were called Sufis adopted the gerund form *tasawwuf*, which means "being a Sufi" or "Sufism," as an appropriate designation for their activities and aspirations. However, these same people also called themselves by other names, such as "knowers" and "ascetics" and "renouncers" and "poor men." What is peculiar about the term Sufi is that its derivation is not completely clear, so it took on the aura of a proper name. But, even if the name was new, the focus and interests of the Sufis were not by any means new. The "reality," as Bushanji points out, was there from Islam's beginning.

In general, the Sufis have looked upon themselves as those Muslims who take seriously God's call to perceive His presence both in the world and in the self. They stress inwardness over outwardness, contemplation over action, spiritual development over legalism, and cultivation of the soul over social interaction. On the theological level, Sufis speak of God's mercy, gentleness, and beauty far more than they discuss His wrath, severity, and majesty. Sufism has been associated both with specific institutions and individuals and with a rich literature.

Given the difficulty of providing an exact definition of Sufism, it is not easy to discern which Muslims have been Sufis and which have not. Being a Sufi certainly has nothing to do with the Sunni/Shi'ite split, nor with the fact that all Muslims are affiliated with one or another of the schools of jurisprudence. Sufism has no special connection with geography, though it has played a greater role in some areas than in others. It has nothing to do with ethnicity, since Sufism is found in all regions of the Islamic world, from Senegal and Albania to China and Indonesia. It has nothing to do with social class, although some Sufi organizations may be more or less class specific. There is no necessary correlation with family. Whole families may be affiliated with a Sufi order, but it is also common to find individuals who profess a Sufi affiliation despite the hostility of family members, or people who have been born into a family of Sufis and consider it an unacceptable form of Islam. Both men and, less commonly, women, become Sufis, and even children participate in Sufi ritual activities, though they are seldom accepted as full-fledged initiates before puberty. Sufism is closely associated with popular religion, but it has also produced the most elite expressions of Islamic teachings. It is often seen as opposed to the state-supported jurists, yet some jurists have always been counted among its devotees, and Sufism in its own turn has frequently been supported by the state along with jurisprudence, or as a counterweight to the influence of the jurists. The characteristic

Sufi institutions – the "orders" or "paths" (*tariqa*) – did not begin to play a major role in Islamic history until about the twelfth century, but even after that time Sufism does not necessarily entail affiliation with an order.

A working description

Specialists in the study of Sufism have reached no consensus as to what they are studying. Those who take seriously the self-understanding of the Sufi authorities usually picture Sufism as an essential component of Islam. Those who are hostile toward Sufism, or hostile toward Islam but sympathetic toward Sufism, or skeptical of any self-understanding by the objects of their study, typically describe Sufism as a movement that was added to Islam after the prophetic period. The diverse theories of Sufism's nature and origins proposed by modern scholars cannot be summarized here, though they do make up a fascinating chapter in the history of Orientalism.

For our purposes, it is enough to repeat that most of Sufism's own theoreticians have understood it to be the living spirit of the Islamic tradition. Ghazali (d. 1111), one of the greatest of the Sufi teachers, gave a nutshell description of Sufism's role in the very title of his magnum opus, *Ihya' ulum ad-din* – "Giving Life to the Sciences of the Religion."

By "sciences" Ghazali means the various branches of learning that had proliferated in Islam after the Prophet. One can say that Islam's root is the Koran and its stem is the Sunnah – the exemplary teachings and practices of the Prophet. As Islam gradually developed into a sturdy tree, its root and stem grew and were strengthened by constantly supplying the Islamic community with sustenance. At the same time, the basic concerns delineated by the Koran and the Sunnah came to be investigated and elaborated upon by different groups of Muslims with varying aptitudes, talents, and goals. They saw the Koran and Sunnah as repositories of teachings and practices that can only be understood and assimilated by careful attention to the tradition handed down from the earliest Muslims. However, each group tended to highlight some aspects of this tradition rather than others.

The Hadith of Gabriel provides one way of analyzing the structure of the tree. In the original root and stem – the Koran and Sunnah – all three dimensions of the religion were inextricably joined. But, as the tree flourished and grew, various branches or sciences grew up from the single root and stem. As we have seen, the three main branches are *islam,* "submission" or correct activity; *iman,* "faith" or correct understanding; and *ihsan,* "doing what is beautiful" – spontaneous virtue and spiritual perfection.

To the extent that Muslims have assimilated their own tradition, they have become involved in all three branches of Islam. Nonetheless, each branch came to have its own great authorities and major exponents, all of whom looked back to the root and the trunk as the primary source of their knowledge, goals, and practices. Only those who spoke for the branch of *ihsan* maintained that *islam* and *iman* must be subordinated to the highest goal, which is "to worship God as if you see him." By and large, such people were associated with what has come to be known as "Sufism." In contrast, those who asserted the primacy of *islam* focused their energies on Sharia and jurisprudence, and those who felt that *iman* and understanding were the foundation of Islam tunneled their efforts into Kalam and other schools of thought that dealt with understanding and expressing the objects of faith. In his "Giving Life to the Sciences of the Religion" Ghazali illustrates in copious detail how *islam* and *iman* need to be vivified and validated by *ihsan.*

The life-giving science of Sufism explains the rationale for both faith and submission. It differs from Kalam both in perspective and focus, but it is no less carefully grounded in the sources of the tradition. On the practical level, Sufism provides the means whereby Muslims can strengthen their understanding and observance of Islam with a view toward finding God in themselves and the world. It intensifies Islamic ritual life through careful attention to the details of the Sunnah and by focusing on *dhikr,* the remembrance of God, at every moment.

Remembrance typically takes the form of the methodical repetition of certain names of God or Koranic formulas, such as the first Shahadah. In communal gatherings, Sufis have usually performed *dhikr* aloud, often with musical accompaniment. In some Sufi groups, these communal sessions came to be considered the most important ritual, with a corresponding neglect of various other aspects of the Sunnah. At this point, Sufi practice became suspect not only in the eyes of the jurists, but also in the eyes of many of the Sufi teachers themselves.

In historical terms, it is helpful to think of Sufism on two levels. On the first level – which is the primary concern of the Sufis – Sufism has no history, because it is an invisible, animating presence within the community of the faithful. On the second level – which concerns both Muslim observers and modern historians – Sufism's presence makes itself known through certain characteristics of people and society or certain specific institutional forms. Wilfred Cantwell Smith, in his well-known critique of the historical study of religion, *The Meaning and End of Religion,* calls these two levels "faith" and "cumulative tradition." They can easily be compared with what Bushanji called the "reality" and the "name" of Sufism. Although Sufi teachings and practices are part of the name and the cumulative tradition, they address the task of awakening faith and opening up the road to experiencing the reality behind the name, which is the living presence of God that animates the tradition.

Like most other Muslims, Sufis had little interest in the "history" of Islam per se. What was important was the teachings of the past that had accumulated in the present. The teachings were studied as an aid to bring to life the religion's ideals and to embody them through everyday activity. Although modern scholars have often claimed to have a disinterested approach to the study of history, they have always described and analyzed the cumulative tradition in terms of their own theories and categories. No doubt such scholarship performs a useful task, but it should not lead observers to forget that Muslims and Sufis have always looked at the cumulative tradition as the surface of an inner reality, as a means and not an end, as the west and not the east. Rumi seems to be addressing the modern scholars when he says,

> Having seen the form, you are unaware of the meaning.
> If you are wise, pick out the pearl from the shell![1]

Those Sufi authors who studied the great figures of the past did so in order to show how exemplary Muslims achieved the goal of human life, which in their view was to live in the divine presence. Hence their typical genre was hagiography, which aims at describing the extraordinary human qualities of those who achieve nearness to God. In contrast, Muslim opponents of Sufism have been anxious to illustrate that Sufism is a distortion of Islam, and they were happy to seize on every opportunity to show that figures known as "Sufis" ignored the essentials of Islam, conspired with unbelief and heresy, and immersed themselves in moral laxity.

The internal, Islamic attacks on Sufism that have often been made over history have many causes. Not least has been the social and political influence of Sufi teachers, which often threatened the power and privileges of the jurists and even the rulers. Moreover, even though the great Sufi authorities set down guidelines for keeping Sufism squarely at the heart of the Islamic tradition, popular religious movements sometimes appeared that were aimed at intensifying religious experience with little concern for Islamic norms, and these frequently became associated with Sufism or grew out of certain sorts of Sufi teachings and practices. Whether or not the members of these movements considered themselves Sufis, opponents of Sufism were happy to claim that their excesses represented Sufism's true nature. The Sufi teachers themselves frequently criticized false Sufis, and the dangers connected with loss of contact with the living core of Islam could only increase when much of Sufism became institutionalized through the Sufi orders.[2]

If, as the great Sufi teachers maintain, Sufism is essentially Islam's living heart, those who study specific historical phenomena have the problem of how to judge the degree to which these phenomena deserve the name. The Sufi teachers typically hold that criteria for authentic Sufism are found in correct activity and correct understanding, and these pertain to the very definition of the religion. In other words, Sufism has to be judged in terms of its adherence to the Koran, the Sunnah, and the consensus of the *ulama';* or, in terms of its ability to actualize the fullness of *islam, iman,* and *ihsan.*

Like other branches of Islamic learning and praxis, Sufism is passed on to disciples from a master, who is typically called a "shaykh" (literally, "old man," "elder"). The shaykh's oral teachings give life to the articles of faith, and without his transmission the methodical practice of *dhikr* is considered invalid if not dangerous. As with Hadith, transmission is traced back through a chain of authorities (called *silsila*) *to* the Prophet. The typical rite of initiation is modeled on the handclasp known as *bay'at ar-ridwan* ("the oath-taking of God's good pleasure") that the Prophet took from his Companions at Hudaybiyya (referred to in Koran 48:10 and 48:18). The rite is understood to transmit an invisible spiritual force or blessing (*baraka*) that opens up the disciple's soul to transformation. The master's fundamental concern − as in other forms of Islamic learning − is to shape the character (*khuluq*) of the disciple so that it conforms to the prophetic model.

If molding the character of students and disciples was a universal concern of Islamic learning, the Sufis developed a science of human nature that had no parallels in jurisprudence or Kalam, though the philosophers knew something similar. So central was shaping character to the Sufi path that Ibn Arabi could define Sufism as "assuming the character traits of God."[3] God created human beings in His own image, and they accepted to carry the Trust, so it is their duty to actualize the divine character traits that are latent in their souls. They cannot do so without the help of teachers who know exactly what these traits are and how to bring them into the open. This concern to bring out the soul's innate divine qualities helps explain the great attention that Sufi teachers devote to the "stations" (*maqamat*) of ascent on the path to God and the "states" (*ahwal*) or psychological and spiritual transformations that travelers undergo in their attempt to pass through the stations.

Sufi theory offered theological teachings that were far more attractive to the vast majority of Muslims than Kalam, which was a rarefied academic discipline with little impact on most people. From the beginning, the Kalam experts attempted to understand Koranic teachings in rational terms with the help of the Greek philosophical heritage. In keeping with the inherent tendency of reason to discern and differentiate, Kalam fastened on all those Koranic verses that assert the transcendence and otherness of God. When faced with verses that assert God's immanence and presence, Kalam explained them away through forced interpretations (*ta'wil*). As Gibb has pointed out, "The more developed theological systems were largely negative and substituted for the vivid personal relation between God and man presented by the Koran an abstract and depersonalized discussion of logical concepts."[4]

The Koran speaks of God with a wide variety of adjectives that it often calls the "most beautiful names." For the most part,

Kalam stresses those divine names that assert God's severity, grandeur, distance, and aloofness. Although many early expressions of Sufism went along with the dominant attitudes in Kalam, another strand of Sufi thinking gradually gained strength and became predominant by the eleventh or twelfth century. This perspective focused on divine attributes that speak of nearness, sameness, similarity, concern, compassion, and love. The Sufi teachers emphasized the personal dimensions of the divine-human relationship, agreeing with the Kalam authorities that God was distant, but adding that His simultaneous nearness was the more important consideration. The grand theological theme of the Sufi authors is epitomized in the hadith of God's precedent mercy, which the Sufis understood to mean that God's nearness is more real than His distance. God is always present, and the perception of His absence will eventually disappear.

If Kalam and jurisprudence depended on reason to establish categories and distinctions, the Sufis depended on another faculty of the soul to bridge gaps and make connections. Many of them called this faculty "imagination" (khayal). For them, it is the innate ability of the soul to perceive the presence of God in all things – a presence indicated by the verse, "Wherever you turn, there is the face of God" (2:115). They found a reference to imagination's power in the Prophet's definition of ihsan – "It is to worship God as if you see Him." Through methodical concentration on the face of God as revealed in the Koran, the Sufis strengthen the "as if" with the aim of reaching the stage of "unveiling" (kashf), which is the generic term for suprarational vision of God's presence in the world and the soul. Ibn Arabi asserts that unveiling is a mode of knowledge superior to reason, but he also insists that reason provides the indispensable checks and balances without which it is impossible to differentiate among divine, angelic, psychic, and satanic inrushes of imaginal knowledge.

Spectrums of theory and practice

Islam's theological axiom, *tawhid*, declares that God is one, but it also asserts that the world is many. All of Islamic theological thinking addresses the issue of how to correlate multiplicity with unity. Those who look more at the divine side of things place greater stress on unity, and those who look more at the world emphasize multiplicity. As a general rule, rational thinking about God focuses on His separation from the world and the world's utter difference from His unique reality, and hence it highlights multiplicity and diversity. In contrast, imagistic or "imaginal" thinking about God tends to see the immanent unity established by God's presence in all things.

A creative tension has existed between these two basic ways of looking at God throughout Islamic history. By and large, the Kalam authorities and jurists have emphasized the rational perception of God's distance, and the Sufis have countered with the imaginal perception of God's nearness. The theologians assert that God is utterly "incomparable" (*tanzih*) with all things in the universe, and the Sufis respond that all things are "similar" (*tashbih*) to Him, because they derive all their reality from Him.[5] Sometimes the balance between these two standpoints has been broken by a stern and exclusivist legal-mindedness on the one hand or an excessively emotional religiosity on the other. In the first case, the understanding of the inner realms of Islamic life is lost, and nothing is left but theological bickering, legalistic nit-picking, and political jockeying for power. In the second case, the necessity for the divine guidance provided by the Sharia is forgotten, and the resulting sectarian movements break off from Islam's mainstream. In modern times, these two extremes are represented by certain forms of "fundamentalism" on one side and deracinated Sufism on the other.[6]

Within the theory and practice of Sufism itself, a parallel differentiation of perspectives can be observed. Many Sufis vigorously asserted God's omnipresent and immanent oneness and the possibility of union with Him. Others stressed His absolute transcendence and emphasized the duties of servant-hood that arise as soon as we distinguish between Creator and creature. Real and unreal, truth and falsehood, right and wrong.

In order to describe the psychological concomitants of these two standpoints, the Sufis spoke of various pairs of "states" (*ahwal*) experienced by the travelers on the path to God. One of the most instructive of these is "intoxication" (*sukr*) and "sobriety" (*sahw*). Intoxication follows upon being overcome by the presence of God. It designates the joy of the seekers in finding the eternal source of all beauty and love within themselves. The travelers see God in all things and lose the ability to discriminate between Him and creation or to differentiate between correct and incorrect. Intoxication is associated with expansion, hope, and intimacy with God. It is the human response to the divine names that declare God's compassion, love, kindness, beauty, gentleness, and concern.[7]

In contrast, sobriety allows for a clear differentiation between God and the world and a calm and careful discernment between right and wrong, beautiful and ugly. It correlates with the absolute distinction between Creator and creatures and is associ-ated with wonderment, awe, contraction, and fear. It is the human response to divine names that designate God's majesty, glory, splendor, magnificence, might, wrath, and vengeance.

If perceiving God's aloofness allows for a clear understanding of the difference between servant and Lord, seeing His nearness blinds the discerning powers of reason. Neither standpoint is complete in itself. The vision of things as they truly are demands a balance between seeing God distant and finding Him near, or between rational understanding and imaginal unveiling.

The contrast between sober and drunk, or between the vision of differentiated multiplicity and the experience of all-embracing unity, reverberates throughout Sufi writing and is reflected in the hagiographical accounts of the Sufi masters. Those who experience intimate oneness are boldly confident of God's mercy, and those who experience awe-inspiring distance remain wary of His wrath. By and large, drunken Sufis tend to de-emphasize the Sharia and declare union with God openly, whereas sober Sufis observe the courtesy (*adab*) of a servant's relationships with his Lord. The sober fault the drunk for disregarding the Sunnah, and the drunk fault the sober for forgetting the overriding reality of God's mercy. Those who, in Ibn Arabi's terms, "see with both eyes" keep reason and unveiling in perfect balance while acknowledging the rights of both sober and drunk.

Expressions of sobriety and intoxication often have rhetorical purposes. Sufis wrote for the purpose of edification, and different teachers attempted to inculcate psychological and spiritual attitudes depending upon the needs they perceived in their listeners and readers. Those authors who disregarded rational norms were not necessarily overcome by the divine wine – if they had been, they would hardly have put pen on paper. So also, sober expressions of Sufism do not mean that the authors knew nothing of intoxication. There is a higher sort of sobriety that sees everything in its proper place and is achieved *after* intoxication, not before it.

Drunken expressions of Sufism predominate in poetry, which is ideally suited to describe the imaginal realm of unveiled, unitary knowledge. Sober expressions find their natural home in prose, which is perfectly suited for the theological abstractions and legal analyses that are the forte of reason. Sufi poetry constantly celebrates God's presence, and Sufi prose tends toward systematic exposition of doctrine and practice, always keeping one eye on the opinions of the jurists and the Kalam experts. Drunken Sufism rarely demonstrates interest in juridical issues or theological debates, whereas sober Sufism offers methodical discussions of all sorts of juridical and theological issues that can quickly prove tiring to any but those trained in the

Islamic sciences. The poets address the highest concerns of the soul and employ the most delicious and enticing imagery. The theoreticians discuss details of practice, behavior, moral development, Koranic exegesis, and the nature of God and the world.

Poetic license allows the Sufi poets to convey the experience of God's presence with imagery that shocks the conventionally pious and flies in the face of juridical and theological discourse. In the best examples, such as Ibn al-Farid in Arabic, Attar, Rumi, and Hafiz in Persian, and Yunus Emre in Turkish, simply hearing the poetry – especially when well recited or sung – gives rise to a marvelous joy.[8] The drunken Sufism of the poets has always been popular among Muslims of all classes and persuasions, and even the most literal-minded jurists are likely to enjoy the poetry's beauty while condemning the ideas.

Sober Sufism tends to attract the more educated practitioners, who are willing to devote long hours to studying texts that are no easier than works on jurisprudence, Kalam, or philosophy. It should not be surprising that for many Westerners, whether scholars or would-be practitioners, "real" Sufism has been identified with the drunken varieties that ignore the hard-nosed concerns of "orthodox" Islam. It is often forgotten that many of those who express themselves in the daring poetry of union also write the respectful prose of separation and servanthood.

Within Sufism's diverse forms, a wide range of perspectives is observable. Some Sufis stress unity, others multiplicity; some love, others knowledge; some intoxication, others sobriety. For the tradition to remain whole, it needs to keep a balance between sobriety and drunkenness, reason and unveiling, concern for the Sharia and Islamic doctrine on the one hand and for the experience of God's presence on the other. If sobriety is lost, so also is rationality, and along with it the strictures of *islam* and *iman,* the formal supports of the cumulative tradition. If drunkenness is lost, so also is religious experience and lived faith, along with love, compassion, and *ihsan.*

The classic example of the contrast between drunken and sober Sufism is found in the pictures drawn of the tenth century figures Hallaj and Junayd. The first became Sufism's great martyr because of his open avowal of the mysteries of divine union and his disregard for the niceties of Shariite propriety. The second, known as the "master of the whole tribe" (*shaykh at-ta'ifa*), kept coolly sober despite achieving the highest degree of union with God.

Another example can be found in the contrast between the two literary high points of the Sufi tradition, Ibn Arabi and Jalal ad-Din Rumi. The former wrote voluminously in Arabic prose and addressed every theoretical issue that arises in the context of Islamic thought and practice. His works are enormously erudite and exceedingly difficult, and only the most learned of Muslims, those already trained in jurisprudence, Kalam, and other Islamic sciences, could have hoped to read and understand them. In contrast, Rumi wrote over 70,000 verses of intoxicating poetry in a language that any Persian-speaking Muslim could understand. He sings constantly of the trials of separation from the Beloved and the joys of union with Him. Nonetheless, the contrast between these two authors should not suggest that Rumi was anti-rational or unlearned, or that Ibn Arabi was not a lover of God and a poet. Rather, we are dealing with two modes of human perfection that yield differences in perspective, rhetorical means, and emphasis, despite a unity of purpose. Among Western scholars, Henry Corbin argues forcefully that Rumi and Ibn Arabi belong to the same group of *fidèles d'amour*.[9]

In the classical Sufi texts, there are two basic and complementary ways of describing Sufism. If the drunken side of Sufism is stressed, it is pictured as disdainful toward jurisprudence and Kalam. If sobriety is stressed, it is viewed as the inner life (*ihsan*) of right practice (*islam*) and right faith (*iman*). The great theoreticians of Sufism speak from the viewpoint of sobriety and strive to establish a balance among all dimensions of Islamic thought and practice, with Sufism as the animating spirit of the whole. Famous names of Sufis in this category include Sarraj (d. 988), Kalabadhi (d. 990), Sulami (d. 1021), Qushayri (d. 1072), Hujwiri (d. 1072), Ghazali (d. 1111), Shihab ad-Din Umar Suhrawardi (d. 1234), Ibn Arabi (d. 1240), Najm ad-Din Razi (d. 1256), and Izz ad-Din Kashani (d. 1334-35). In contrast, the everyday practice of Sufism, especially in its popular dimensions, tends to appear in an antagonistic mode with legalistic Islam, even though this is by no means always the case.[10]

Sufism in the modern world

In the nineteenth and twentieth centuries, many Muslims have sought a revival of authentically Islamic teachings and practices, not least in order to fend off Western political and cultural domination. Some Muslims have responded largely in political terms, others have tried to revive Islam's inner life. Among most of the Western-educated and politically minded, Sufism became the scapegoat through which Islam's "backwardness" could be explained. In this view, Sufism is the religion of the common people and embodies superstitious elements brought in from other religions or local cultures. In order for Islam to reclaim its birthright, which in the eyes of such critics includes modern science and technology, Sufism must be eradicated.

Until recently, most Western observers have considered reformers of this type to be "Islam's hope to enter the modern age." Nowadays, however, the dissolution of Western cultural identity and an awareness of the ideological roots of ideas such as progress and development have left the rabid modernists looking naive, though certainly dangerous. In the meantime, various Sufi teachers have kept themselves busy reviving the Islamic heritage by focusing upon what they consider the root cause of every disorder – forgetfulness of God. Especially interesting here is the case of the famous Algerian freedom fighter, Abd al-Qadir Jaza'iri (d. 1883), who devoted his exile in Syria to reviving the heritage of Ibn Arabi. Today grass-roots Islam is far more likely to be inspired by Sufi teachers than by modernist intellectuals, who are cut off from the masses because of their Western-style academic training. However, the presence in most Islamic societies of demagogues who have no qualms about manipulating religious sentiment for political ends complicates the picture immensely.

Parallel to the resurgence of Sufism in the Islamic world has been the spread of Sufi teachings to the West. Drunken Sufism was introduced in the early part of this century by the Indian shaykh and musician, Inayat Khan. His teachings have been continued by his son, Pir Vilayet Inayat Khan, a frequent lecturer on the New Age circuit. In France, sober Sufism gained a wide audience among intellectuals through the writings of the mathematician turned metaphysician Rene Guenon, also known as Shaykh Abd al-Wahid, who died in Cairo in 1951.

More recently Western languages have seen the publication of hundreds of volumes addressed to seekers of God and reflecting the range of perspectives found in the original texts, from extreme sobriety to utter intoxication. Many of these works are written by authentic representatives of Sufi *silsilas,* while many more are written by people who have adopted Sufism to justify teachings of questionable origin, or who have left the safeguards of right practice and right thought – *islam* and *iman* – and hence have no access to the *ihsan* that is built on the two.

Contemporary representatives of sober Sufism emphasize knowledge, discernment, and differentiation, and they usually stress the importance of observing the Sharia. Best known in this group is Frithjof Schuon, who was a shaykh of the Shadhiliyya-Alawiyya order of North Africa, though he lived most of his life in Switzerland and the United States. He takes an extreme position on the importance of discernment and offers a rigorous criticism of the roots of modern anti-religion. The main thrust of his writings seems to be to offer a theory of world religions based on the idea of a universal "esoterism," the Islamic form of which is Sufism. He frequently asserts the necessity for "esoterists" of all religions to observe the practical, "exoteric" dimension of their own traditions, this being the Sharia in the case of Islam. Martin Lings, who has also published under the name Abu Bakr Siraj ed-Din, presents a picture of Sufism that is intellectually rigorous but strongly grounded in Islamic texts. The noted Iranian scholar Seyyed Hossein Nasr also stresses intellectual discernment more than love, and he repeatedly insists that there is no Sufism without the Sharia.

The books of the Turkish Cerrahi leader Muzaffer Ozak present Sharia-oriented Sufism that is much more focused on love than on intellectual discernment. The Naqshbandi master Nazim al-Qubrusi offers a warm presentation of desirable human qualities, again rooted in a perspective that stresses love and often discusses the Shariite basis of Sufism. The Iranian Ni'matallahi leader Dr. Javad Nurbakhsh has published several excellent anthologies of classic Sufi texts. His own perspective falls on the side of intoxication, with emphasis on oneness of being and union with God. He pays little attention to the Sharia, but discusses the importance of Sufi communal activities such as sessions of *dhikr*. Even more to the side of love and intoxication are the works of Guru Bawa Muhaiyaddeen, who presents a synthesis of Sufism and various Hindu teachings.

3
Name and reality

Sufism is an unsatisfactory and often controversial name that has come to be applied to various social and institutional manifestations of the inner reality of Islamic faith. It is a name that some have considered a badge of honor and others a term of opprobrium. Enough has already been said about the name, however. To get closer to the reality, we need to look at other names and other descriptions.

One of the terms often used in the classical texts to designate what I call "Sufism" is *ma'rifa* (or *irfan*), a term that literally means "knowledge" or "recognition." However, the term connotes a special, deeper knowledge of things that can only be achieved by personal transformation, and hence it is often translated as "gnosis." The goal and fruit of this type of knowledge is commonly explained by citing the Prophet's saying, "He who knows [*arafa*] himself knows his Lord." As the hadith suggests, this sort of knowledge demands a simultaneous acquisition of both self-knowledge and God-knowledge. The texts tell us repeatedly that it cannot be found in books. Rather, it is already present in the heart, but it is hidden deep beneath the dross of ignorance, forgetfulness, outwardly oriented activity, and rational articulation. Access to this knowledge comes only by following the path that leads to human perfection.

Generally speaking, those who have become famous in the West as Sufis – such as Hallaj, Rumi, and Ibn Arabi – represent a few of the more outstanding Muslims who have spoken for this dimension of the religion, or for the full actualization of self-knowledge. But it should be kept in mind that despite the constant publication of Sufi texts throughout the Islamic world since the introduction of printing, the vast majority of Sufi writings have never been published, and even those that have been published remain largely unstudied and unread. The literature is vast, and the modern interest is scant, especially among contemporary Muslims. For every Hallaj who has been studied in modern times, there are dozens of other major figures waiting to be investigated. Moreover, the literature that has been written by the Sufis, or about the Sufis, represents only a tiny fraction of the phenomenon of Sufism, since the great majority of Muslims who devoted themselves to God – including most of those who were known in their own time or by later generations as great Sufis or gnostics – did not have the vocation of writing. The literary output represents only the name of a much deeper and broader reality that by nature cannot be known from the outside.

The expression of Sufi teachings

I said earlier that "theoretical Sufism" represents one of the three main approaches to faith or understanding. I suggested that Sufi theory is different from other theorizing because it emphasizes imaginal perception rather than rational investigation. We can also say that what differentiates the Sufi approach to Islamic faith is the stress on *ma'rifa* – the direct knowledge of self and God that flows freely in the purified heart. In contrast, the other two approaches to faith, Kalam and philosophy, affirm the necessity of *ilm*, which can be translated as knowledge, science, or learning. They insist that the primary means of gaining knowledge is reason (*aql*), and the theologians add that reason has to submit to the givens of revelation.

Like the Kalam experts and unlike the philosophers, the Sufis gave pride of place to the Koran and the Hadith, but they also held that the only way to understand the revelatory message was to purify the heart so that it would be worthy of being taught by

God Himself. They liked to quote the Koranic verse, "Be wary of God, and God will teach you" (2:282). Since "being wary of God" (*taqwa*) is designated by the Koran itself (49:13) as the highest human attribute in God's eyes, this verse was a powerful scriptural support for their position. Abu Yazid Bastami, a ninth-century figure commonly called the "sultan of the gnostics," is reported to have said to certain scholars who were objecting to his formulations of Islamic teachings, "You take your knowledge dead from the dead, but I take my knowledge from the Living who does not die."

As noted earlier, the Sufis commonly called this direct knowledge of God "unveiling." Partly because unveiling often takes the form of a visionary, imagistic knowledge, they made frequent use of poetry to express their teachings about God, the world, and the human soul. Many of them felt that poetry was the ideal medium for expressing the truths of the most intimate and mysterious relationship that human beings can achieve with God, that is, loving Him and being loved by Him. In Islamic civilization in general, poetry is the most important literary form, and it has always been widely popular among both the literate and illiterate classes. In most of the Islamic world – that is, wherever Arabic was not the mother tongue – the various poetical traditions of the Islamic languages were far more important for propagating the world view of the Koran than the Koran itself. And most of the really great and popular poets were either Sufi masters or spokesmen for Sufi teachings.

It was noted that the Sufi approach to explaining the Koran's message stresses the nearness, presence, and immanence of God rather than His distance and transcendence. There are many Koranic verses to support this position, such as, "And We are nearer to him than the jugular vein" (50:16), or "And He is with you wherever you are" (57:4). The general position of the theologians was to interpret these verses as metaphors so as to emphasize God's transcendence and to remove any suggestion of a personal nearness. In contrast, the Sufis thought that such "anthropomorphic" verses should not be taken as mere metaphors, but rather as statements of the actual situation – though they never fell into the trap of ignoring the complementary teaching, that of God's distance and transcendence.

Sufi attempts to balance the demands of transcendence and immanence help explain why they are especially fond of paradoxes – statements that express subtle truths by ignoring the law of non-contradiction. These help break down the insistence of the rational mind that everything can be explained and grasped. In fact God does not fit into our categories. Everything in our world and our experience must be one thing or another, but God is both nothing and everything. He is both near and far, both transcendent and immanent, both absent and present, both this and not this.

Many Sufis maintain, in fact, that true understanding of God can only be achieved through perplexity and bewilderment. The paradoxical and sometimes scandalous utterances that tend to emerge at this loss of rational distinctions manifest inner awe, wonder, and astonishment. One of the favorite Sufi expressions of perplexity goes back to Abu Bakr, the close companion of the Prophet and the first caliph after his death – "Incapacity to perceive is perception." We perceive the things of this world by perceiving them, but we perceive God by the clear perception that we do not and cannot perceive Him.

The Sufis who stress paradox and bewilderment tend to fall on the side of intoxication, while those who speak in more measured terms keep their sobriety. The eye of imagination, unveiling, and gnosis revels in God's presence and throws away all pretensions to sober judgment and logical precision. The eye of reason knows nothing of God's presence, because its analytical approach can only dissect endlessly and reach the conclusion that God is nowhere to be found.

In the frequent discussions of the relative virtues of sobriety and drunkenness, teachers often speak of three stages on the path. Before entering the path itself, most people appear to be sober but are actually drunk. This is blameworthy sobriety, because it grows up from being drunk and deluded by the illusory standards of social reality, the trappings and goals of ordinary life. Such sobriety is a mortal danger for the soul, because it is built on forgetfulness of God and heedlessness of the human situation. When people enter the Sufi path, they reach true sobriety by turning away from the follies of this world and coming to their senses.

After long struggle on the path of discipline and self-purification, the seekers may be opened up to the effusions of divine love, mercy, and knowledge. This can be so overwhelming that they lose their powers of rational discernment and tend to express themselves in ecstatic and paradoxical language. This is the stage of true intoxication, but it is not the final stage of the path. Neither the Prophet nor the vast majority of the great Muslims who followed in his footsteps were drunk. They had reached the still-further stage, "sobriety after drunkenness," which is the return to the world after the journey to God. In traveling to God, the seekers undergo total transformation, but now they come back with helping hands. They began as stones, they were shattered by the brilliance of the divine light, and now they have been resurrected as precious jewels – beautiful, luminous, and fixed in the divine attributes.

The two higher stages of this tripartite scheme – that is, "intoxication" and "sobriety after intoxication" – correlate with the famous expressions *fana'* and *baqa'*, or "annihilation" and "subsistence." Through the journey of self-purification and devotion to God, the travelers reach a stage where they become fully open to the divine light, and the brilliance of this light annihilates all the human limitations that had held them back from seeing their true selves and their Lord. The annihilation of obstacles and impediments allows them to see that they themselves had been nothing and still are nothing, because God alone has true reality. Instead of themselves, who had never had any reality to speak of, they now see what subsists after the annihilation of idols and false selfhood. What remains is precisely God in His glory, and this glory demands the shining of His light. According to Rumi's interpretation of Hallaj's scandalous utterance, this is the stage at which he said, "I am the Real."

The terms *annihilation* and *subsistence* are derived from the Koranic passage, "Everything upon the earth is undergoing annihilation, but there subsists the face of your Lord, Possessor of Majesty and Generous Giving" (55:26–27). The specific divine name with which this verse ends – "Possessor of Majesty and Generous Giving" – is especially appropriate in the context of the spiritual journey, because it alludes to the two-sided perception of things that needs to be achieved. God is the "Possessor of Majesty," because He is Great, Distant, Wrathful, Vengeful, King, and Transcendent. His majesty and splendor are such that they annihilate the reality and existence of everything else. Only He is truly worthy to exist. But God is also "Possessor of Generous Giving," because He is Loving, Merciful, Compassionate, Gentle, Clement, Kind, and Nurturing, and He does nothing but give generously to His creatures. Although His majestic reality annihilates the creatures, His generous bestowal gives them a new reality and true subsistence.

In other terms, annihilation results from the negation asserted in the first half of the first Shahadah, and subsistence from the affirmation mentioned in the second half. "No god" demands that all the positive qualities and characteristics that are ascribed to creatures be negated from them, because in truth these do not belong to them. "But God" means that God alone can be affirmed as real, so every positive attribute and quality belongs only to Him. When the travelers reach the perfection of their own capacity, created in God's image, they experience nothing but the negation of egocentric, separative reality and the affirmation of God-centered, unitive reality.

In contrasting subsistence and annihilation, we need to remember that subsistence is real, not annihilation, for subsistence is the affirmation of an ancient reality, but annihilation is the negation of something that never truly was. "No god" negates all false realities, and "but God" affirms the subsistence of the Real. In terms of the divine attributes, this means that the mercy that designates God's presence and sameness dominates over the wrath that expresses His absence and otherness. God's mercy takes precedence over His wrath, so mercy and subsistence have the final say, not wrath and annihilation.

Divine and human love

Although sobriety represents the highest stage of the Sufi path, this does not imply that the sober are no longer drunk. What it means is that the true Sufi, having realized fully the pattern and model established by the Prophet, is inwardly drunk with God and outwardly sober with the world. Of course, the joy of intoxication may occasionally appear outwardly, but the sobriety of discernment remains a necessary concomitant of faith. The world is the domain of doing what is right and proper, and this needs to be established in terms of a clear distinction between do's and don'ts. Observing the necessary distinctions demands sober awareness of our actual situation in the world and society. Inwardly, however, those who have reached sobriety after drunkenness revel in the intimacy of living with God.

Intoxication is the fruit of finding God. The Sufis commonly express the quest for God in the language of love, the most intense and profound of human experiences. In employing this language, they are following not only the realities of human nature, but also explicit Koranic verses and hadiths. Especially significant is this verse: "Say [O Muhammad!]: 'If you love God, follow me, and then God will love you'" (3:31). There is hardly any verse in the Koran more important for specifying the rationale for Islamic and Sufi praxis. Why is it that Muslims strive so hard to follow the Prophet's Sunnah? The simple answer is that they love God and God has commanded them to follow Muhammad so that God may come to love them.

In a typical Sufi reading of this verse, love for God drives the seeker to search for the mutuality of love, which is to say that the lover wants to be loved by his Beloved and to taste the wine of his Beloved's embrace. No lover is satisfied short of reciprocity. The verse tells us that the only way to show that you love God is to adopt the sobriety of Muhammad, and this means that you must follow his practices, that is, the Sunnah, which is codified in the Sharia. If you can sincerely follow Muhammad, that will make you worthy of God's love and open you up to the intoxication of His presence.

In a hadith that is constantly cited in Sufi works, the Prophet describes what happens when lovers of God devote themselves wholly to their Beloved. Such devotion demands two sorts of practice – obligatory and supererogatory, both of which are codified in the Sharia. True lovers can never be satisfied with doing what the Beloved asks and nothing more. They give fully and freely of everything that they hope will please their Beloved. In this authoritative saying, the Prophet quotes God's words concerning the servants who love Him and who follow the Prophet's Sunnah so that God may love them in return.

> My servant draws near to Me through nothing that I love more than what I have made obligatory for him. My servant never ceases drawing near to Me through supererogatory works until I love him. Then, when I love him, I am his hearing with which he hears, his sight with which he sees, his hand with which he grasps, and his foot with which he walks.

Once the seekers love God, they will be loved by Him in return. God's love may then intoxicate them and annihilate all their human failings and limitations. It may drive away the darkness of temporality and contingency, leaving in its place the radiance of God's own eternal being. Note here that the hadith says, "When I love him, *I am* his hearing with which he hears." As some Sufis have pointed out, the words *I am* alert us to the fact that God is already our hearing with which we hear, our sight with which we see, and our hand with which we grasp. The problem is not God's nearness to us, because He is eternally near to us and closer than our jugular vein. The problem is our nearness to God, which we cannot see and cannot fathom. The seeing of God's nearness has to be achieved, and the way to do so is to devote oneself to the Prophetic model. Although we do not see Him now, we can achieve the seeing of Him if we worship and serve Him as if we see Him.

The sobriety of names

"Sufism," Bushanji said, "used to be a reality without a name." When people start naming things, the reality that tends to get lost is the presence of God. Naming brings about a certain distance, differentiation, and sobriety. The Koran tells us that after God created Adam, "He taught him the names, all of them" (2:31). Naming is part of human nature, because God taught people language at the time of their creation. But naming pertains to separation and multiplicity, to the rational discernment that allows us to experience ourselves as different from others. In contrast, the uncreated and undifferentiated realm represents a kind of drunkenness. When lovers find their Beloved present, they lose sight of multiplicity, separation, and otherness, and they cannot tell the difference between themselves and God. Seekers become drunk on the path to God because distinctions blur and they are drowned in the sweet ocean of love's unity, an ocean that knows nothing of creaturely distinctions.

The "names" that God taught to Adam are bodies that God

Himself bestowed on the realities prefigured in His own eternal knowledge. Like all bodies, they pass and perish, but also like all bodies, they have fixed archetypes in the Divine. And just as names are bodies, so also bodies are names for the divine spirit that God breathed into each of His images. Each body provides the spirit with a different name, which is to say that we differentiate reality through our very selves, because we are diverse images of the one God. In the same way, we differentiate things by naming them, because we are Adam's children.

In the Sufi view, the difficulty of our situation arises from the fact that we have forgotten that God taught us the names at the beginning, and that, in order to know the significance of the names, in order to perceive the realities behind the names, we have to know the names as God taught them. This is achieved by loving God rather than by loving the names and what they designate. Loving God is put into practice by following Muhammad. Then God will love us and revivify the names, and then we will see things as they truly are. We will see every name as the designation for a different ray of God's effulgent light.

If Sufism began as a "reality without a name," it was because those Muslims who loved God at the beginning of Islam simply loved God and therefore followed the Prophet, and they in turn were loved by God. They had no need to name what they were doing. They lived in harmony with their Creator by following His designated messenger and guide. But as time passed, people found it more and more difficult to live up to the reality of love, to imitate the Prophet with perfect compliance, and to achieve the state where God was their hearing and their sight, speaking to them about Himself and showing them the signs of His presence in all things. Instead, they spoke more and more about how God's presence was to be achieved, and they named it by a name they themselves devised. The name – whether it be "Sufism" or something else – is perishing and of no real account. The reality, however, is everything.

4
Self-help

Sufi teachers offer coherent descriptions of the cosmos and the soul and explain the trajectory that takes people back to God. Their view of the human situation can be summarized by the hadith, "This world is accursed – accursed is what is within it, save the remembrance of God." Inasmuch as the world and all things within it are isolated from their divine source, they are distorted, dark, and disoriented, because the sun has set. But the same world and the same things, considered as the signs of God, are the shining rays of the risen Sun. The world as west is accursed, but the world as east is a joyful song of remembrance, inciting those who can see to celebrate the blessedness of all things.

In order to learn how to see God in oneself and things, one has to learn how to be aware of God constantly. One has to see the shining light of the risen sun in a landscape that others perceive as shrouded in midnight. All the practices of Islam and Sufism are focused on one goal – allowing people to open up their eyes and see. Numerous Koranic verses and prophetic sayings speak of this goal with a great variety of images and expressions. One of the most succinct of these and one that has often been taken by Sufi teachers as the definition of the path to God is *tazkiyat an-nafs*, a phrase that is usually translated as "purification of the soul."

The phrase is derived from a Koranic verse that I would translate, with some hesitation, as follows: "By the soul and That which shaped it, and inspired it to its depravity and its godwariness. Prosperous is he who purifies it, and failed has he who buries it" (91:7–10). According to this verse, only those who purify their souls achieve "prosperity." The Koranic context makes clear that this prosperity pertains to the next world and that the prosperity of this world is irrelevant, if not positively dangerous. Those who fail to purify their souls and instead "bury" their souls – as if they were hiding their souls under the ground – will not be prosperous. Instead, they will be miserable when they move on to their final home, whether or not they consider themselves prosperous here.

Like all translations of Koranic passages, this translation is problematic and tentative. To begin with, "purify" is definitely a misleading translation for *tazkiya*. All the dictionaries tell us that *tazkiya* has two senses, though the lexicographers disagree as to which sense is more basic. One meaning of the verb is to purify and cleanse, the other to augment and increase. Hence *tazkiyat an-nafs,* as the Koran commentators recognize, can be understood to mean both "purification" of the *nafs* and "augmentation" of the *nafs.* Most commentators stress the first meaning, apparently for theological reasons. After all, the primary task of Muslims is to submit themselves to God, and this cannot happen until they rid themselves of things that God does not like. This can be called "purification." However, it is obvious that the soul also needs to grow and to increase in stature with God's help. Bringing about this growth can also be called *tazkiya*. Thus, two things need to take place, and both are implied in the word *tazkiya* – purification and augmentation. We can also consider purification as occurring simultaneously with the soul's growth and increase, and thus the two senses of the word coalesce.

The complementarity of these two meanings can be seen in some of the ways in which the word *tazkiya* is used. The dictionaries tell us that it can be employed for planting seeds or raising cattle, in which cases it means neither to purify nor to augment, but something that combines these two senses. When seeds are planted in the ground, they are purified of everything alien to them and exposed to God's bounties – earth, water, and sunlight. This prepares the way for the seeds to increase and grow. Those who plant the seeds neither "purify" them nor "augment" them. Rather, they put them into a situation where they can thrive, prosper, and bring out their own potentiality. Hence *tazkiyat an-nafs* means not only "to purify the soul," but also to allow the soul to grow and thrive by opening it up to the bounty of God. A better translation might be "cultivation of the soul."

The human self

The verb *tazkiya* is used twelve times in the Koran. Usually God is the subject and people are the object. In most of these verses, the point is that God's grace and guidance purify and bless people, though, as the just-cited verse shows, people themselves play an important role in the process. In contrast, the Koran uses the word *nafs* almost three hundred times. In many passages, the word is simply a reflexive pronoun, so it can be applied to human beings, to God, and to other things as well. In the reflexive sense, "self" is clearly the best translation. The Koran also uses the term in senses that are not quite reflexive, but the term *self* is still a better translation than *soul*. For example, the Koran quotes Jesus as addressing God with these words: "You," O God, "know what is in my self, but I do not know what is in Your self" (5:116). In addition, the Koran uses the term to refer to the human self in general without any noun to which it is referring back, and in this context translators typically render it as "soul" instead of "self." In short, the word *nafs* in the Koran can often be translated as "soul" and always as "self."

One problem with both "soul" and "self" is that people tend to reify them, the first in particular. In other words, they talk as if the soul were a "thing," with a concrete, distinct reality, much as the body is looked upon as a thing. Thus, for example, people sometimes argue whether or not human beings have souls or whether or not animals have souls. In these debates, souls are typically imagined as concrete and distinct realities, especially when people attempt to explain souls in what they call "scientific" terms. Scientific thinking, by its nature, is near-sighted. It has no possible way to deal with terms like *nafs* as they are used in the Islamic texts. To argue about the existence of the soul in Arabic would sound silly, especially if the word *nafs* were employed, not least because the Arabic language and Koranic usage demand that everything have a *nafs*.

In Koranic terms, the issue is not whether or not human beings have a *nafs*, because everything has a *nafs*. The issue is this: what exactly is a human *nafs*, and how does it differ from God's *nafs*, or from an animal's *nafs*, or from a stone's *nafs*? Why is it that God has no need for *tazkiya* of His *nafs*? Why is it that God does not command any angel or animal to perform *tazkiya* on its *nafs*? Here a Persian proverb points in the right direction. For "beating cold iron," the Persians say, "Reciting Yasin into the ear of a donkey" – Yasin being Chapter 36 of the Koran, which has always been recognized as having special power and blessing. A donkey's *nafs* is profoundly different from a human *nafs*, because, if you recite the Koran into a human ear, it may do some good, but a donkey will never stop being an ass.

What exactly, then, is different about a human *nafs*? The basic Islamic answer to this question is that it is not within our capacity to have any precise and exact answer to this question, or rather, the specific quality of a human *nafs* is that, in its deepest reality, it has *no* specific quality. This needs some explanation.

When we say, "I saw myself in a mirror," we mean we saw the reflection of our physical form. However, the very fact that we recognize ourselves in the mirror shows that there is much more to self than simply physical form. The words *nafs* in Arabic and "self" in English refer to everything that we are, and that includes both our physical body and our awareness of self and others. But what else does it include? It is now commonplace to acknowledge that people are much more than they think they are because they have "unconscious" minds. But where exactly do we draw the boundaries between self and other? The real problem in talking about self is that we do not know what we are and we cannot know what we are in anything more than a rough and ready sense. If we think we know who we are, we are mistaken.

Few people bother to reflect on their own selves, and this is certainly one of the meanings of the key Koranic term *ghafla* or "heedlessness." Those who do reflect upon themselves will either be confused or lying if they say that they have solved the problem of who they are. The well-known novelist Walker Percy develops this point in his *Lost in the Cosmos: The Last Self-Help Book*. In many ways, the book is a parody of all the self-help books that are found on the shelves of the local bookstores (and I'm sure it pleases Percy in his grave that the book is carefully filed among them). The problem, as Percy illustrates, is that none of the people who write these self-help books and none of their readers have the slightest idea what this self is that they are trying to help. Percy provides his book with several subtitles. One of them is worth quoting if only to gain an appreciation of the book's tone: "How you can survive in the Cosmos about which you know more and more while knowing less and less about yourself, this despite 10,000 self-help books, 100,000 psychotherapists, and 100 million fundamentalist Christians."

If close attention is paid to discussions of the *nafs* in Islamic texts, it will be seen that the unknowability of the human self is an underlying theme. Few Muslim authorities make the mistake of reifying the self, since they know that the self has no specific limits. However, especially for those who have not studied these texts carefully, it may not be obvious that the basic Islamic idea of the self is that it is unknown and indefinable. In order to support my contention, let me cite a bit of Koranic evidence.

The very fact that the word *an-nafs*, "the self," is used in a non-reflexive sense to refer only to human beings should tell us that there is a problem knowing what a human being is. The word *nafs*, as I said, can be applied to anything, including God, because it is the reflexive pronoun. Therefore, *nafs* cannot designate any specific thing, since in each case the *nafs* is simply the very thing that was mentioned or implied, whatever it may be. Just as God's self is unique to Himself, each creature's self is also unique to itself, because each *nafs* is simply what the thing is, and no other creature is exactly the same thing, or else the two would be one. God's self is simply God, and a creature's self is simply the creature. I have a self, and it is nothing but me, and you have a self, and it is nothing but you. If there is something peculiar about the human self, it must be that it alone deserves to be designated by the word "self" outside the reflexive context. When the Koran says "the *nafs*," this can only be the human *nafs*. This implies that the indefiniteness of the word *nafs*, which allows it to be ascribed to anything, is so appropriate in the human case that it is the distinguishing characteristic of human beings.

Given that the self is unknown and indefinite, we will not get anywhere by asking, "What is the self?" We cannot reify and specify it. If we want to "purify" the self or "cultivate" the self, it will do us no good to begin by asking what a self is, because we will not find an answer. We can only deal with the issue head-on in personal terms. Instead of asking, "What is the self?", each of us has to ask "Who am I?"

The Koranic answer to this question is indirect, perhaps because God does not want to encourage people to think that they know for sure who they are. However, the Koran makes clear that all of us share certain characteristics with our father Adam. These general characteristics differentiate us from God's self on the one hand and from the self of non-human creatures on the other. The Koran also makes clear that no created self has achieved its final selfhood – if it ever achieves its final selfhood – because each creature dwells in change and flux. Each "I" is in the process of unfolding, and there is no reason to think that this process will ever come to an end. The difference here between the self of human beings and the self of non-human beings is that, with the slightest amount of reflection, every human self knows that it has not yet come to its end. Each of us knows, if we are alive, that our self has not taken its last "breath" (*nafas* – a word that is written exactly the same as *nafs* in Arabic). Other things are not given this sort of self-awareness, so they act without thought and reflection. Recite scripture to asses and you will be wasting your time. But human beings know that they are constantly faced with unknown dimensions of themselves, because they know that they do not know what they will be and what they will do in the next moment.

In many Islamic theological texts, the problem of self-awareness comes up clearly in the issue of free choice. By performing a volitional act, by making a choice, I specify who I am – what my self is – to some degree. Until I make the choice, that moment of my self has not appeared in the world. And of course, here the Koran tells people repeatedly that they will be held responsible for these choices, which is to say that they will have to answer to God when He asks them why they did what they did. They will have to tell God why they chose to make this act appear from their selves and not some other act.

Everyone knows that each of us stands in the midst of development and unfolding. What is being unfolded is simply our self, but each self is unique. We do not know the full answer to what we are because at the moment we are only what we are right now, and at every moment of our existence, we are something new. So what is our self? It is the I of the moment, and each moment is new.

A famous aphorism tells us, "The Sufi is the child of the moment" (*as-sufi ibn al-waqt*). One of its meanings is that the true Sufi lives in the constant awareness that his self is nothing but what he is at the present moment. And since each present moment is unique, each moment of the self is unique. In some Sufi texts, each moment of the self is called a *nafas*, a "breath." The Sufis are then called "the folk of the breaths" (*ahl al-anfas*), because they live in full awareness of the uniqueness of the *nafs* at each *nafas,* each breath, each instant.

What is this new self that we experience at each breath? According to the standard Ash'arite theological view, as refined by numerous disquisitions on the same topic by a variety of Sufi authors, the new self of the moment is God's constant and never-ending renewal of the self's creation. At each moment of our existence, a new self arrives to us from God, just as, in this body, a new breath arrives.

The subsistent face

The Sufis sometimes deal with the constant renewal of self in terms of the notions of *fana'* and *baqa'*, "annihilation" and "subsistence." As noted, the terms refer to the Koranic verse, "Everything upon the earth is undergoing annihilation, but there subsists the face of your Lord" (55:26–27). The self undergoes annihilation at every moment, but the face of God subsists. This "face" is His display of His own names and attributes through the constant and continual creation of the self. In itself, this self has nothing to call its own, because everything it possesses quickly disappears. In truth, individuals have no self other than what they are with God, and all of what they are belongs to God, not to them. Our true and proper self is no self at all, that is, no self of our own. Our true self is the self that God gives to us at each instant, and, since we live in the process of God's everlasting renewal of the self, we will subsist forever in the divine acts and attributes that come to us.

In other terms, our true self is the face of God that looks upon us at each instant of our existence. The Koranic verse that was earlier translated, "Everything is perishing but His face" (28:88) can also be translated "Everything is perishing but *its* face," with the pronoun going back to "everything" instead of God. But the upshot is the same. In the first case, the verse means that all things perish except the face of God, and God's face is that which "looks" upon creation. "Wherever you turn, there is the face of God" (2:115) looking back at you. It is the face of God that gives you whatever reality you have, for, if He did not look at you, you would cease to exist.

If we read the verse as saying that "its face" does not perish, this means that your face does not perish because your face in truth is that which looks upon God, and that can only be the face of God looking back at you, for nothing sees God but God. In *The Niche of Lights*, Ghazali explains that the gnostics see the unperishing face. Then he points out that each thing has two faces, one turned toward itself and one turned toward God. The first face looks toward self, which is the west, and the second toward God, who is the east. Notice that Ghazali begins by contrasting "metaphor" (*majaz*) and "reality" (*haqiqa*). The metaphor is the ray of light, and the reality is the sun.

> The gnostics climb up from the lowlands of metaphor to the highlands of reality, and they perfect their ascent. Then they see by direct eye-witnessing that there is none in existence save God and that *Everything is perishing but His face*. Not that each thing comes to perish at one time rather than another, but rather that it is perishing from eternity without beginning to eternity without end. It cannot be conceived of in any other way. After all, when the essence of anything other than He is considered in respect of its own essence, it is sheer nonexistence. But when it is considered in terms of the face to which existence flows forth from the First, the Real, then it is seen as existing – not in itself, but through the face toward its Giver of Existence. Hence the only existent is the Face of God.

> So, each thing has two faces – a face toward itself, and a face toward its Lord. Considered in terms of the face of itself, it is nonexistent, but considered in terms of the face of God, it exists. Hence, there is no existent but God and His face. Therefore, *Everything is perishing but His face* from eternity without beginning to eternity without end.[1]

"Everything is perishing but the face," which is the true self. So, no self will perish, and every individual human self will subsist forever. However, people have enormously diverse levels of understanding and awareness. Some have no idea what is going on and think that their selves are their own. Some think they do know what is going on. Some live in the face of God and experience the ever-renewed creation with total presence – these last being "the folk of the breaths" or "the children of the moment."

Whatever the level of understanding, everyone needs *tazkiya* – purification and augmentation – of the self. Those who think that their own selves are specific, defined, and limited by their own perceptions and experiences need to purify their selves of heedlessness and ignorance. Those who think they know themselves need to purify and augment their knowledge. And those who experience the ever-renewed self-disclosures of the divine face rejoice in constantly renewed purification and never-ending augmentation. Here we have the common Sufi triad *nafs ammara* (the self that commands [to evil]), *nafs lawwama* (the self that blames [itself for its own shortcomings]), and *nafs mutma'inna* (the self at peace [with God]). These are three basic stages that must be traversed if people are to achieve perfection.

We can also consider this issue in light of the Koranic account of Adam, who is the father of all human beings and the first prophet, the model that each person needs to imitate in order to be fully human. When the Koran says, "God taught Adam the names, all of them" (2:31), one of the basic meanings is simply that human beings have within themselves the potential for infinite knowledge. The name of everything that God has created and will create lies within them. By becoming aware of things in the outside and inside worlds, they gain awareness of the names of things and realize that they have always known them. However, unless they know *all* the names that God taught Adam, they cannot know their own selves. Knowledge of the names is inherent to Adam's self and to the self of each of his children. One might say that it is precisely this knowledge that underlies the Islamic concept of *fitra*, the "original disposition" that allows people to recognize God's unity. If people do not know what God taught to the Adamic self, then they have not known themselves.

If God taught people "*all* the names," as the Koran puts it, how can they ever know these names simultaneously and with full awareness? In fact, it is impossible to actualize the fully differentiated knowledge of the names all at once, because that would mean knowing everything that God has created and will create, and God's creation is in effect infinite. Hence, human beings will continue to actualize the knowledge of the names forever, and this explains the bliss of paradise, which is God's endless and constantly renewed bestowal of awareness on each and every fortunate self. Hell, of course, also involves bestowal of awareness, but awareness does not necessarily bring about happiness. One of the most painful things in the world can be awareness of one's own shortcomings and stupidities. Ibn Arabi tells us that God does not keep people in hell forever in order to punish them, but rather to have mercy on them. They will eventually become accustomed to the torments and even begin to enjoy them, but if they were taken to paradise, they would be embarrassed before God and the prophets, and that would be a much more painful torment than the fires of hell.[2]

In all this I have not forgotten the hadith of self-knowledge,

"He who knows his self knows his Lord." Many interpretations of this saying have been offered, but, however we interpret it, we cannot offer it as proof that we can know ourselves or our Lord completely and totally. Rather, to the extent that we come to know ourselves, to the same extent we will also come to know our Lord. Ibn Arabi reminds us that God in Himself is ultimately unknowable. Jesus did not know what is in God's self, and certainly no one else can claim to know it. Thus Ibn Arabi writes,

> I think – and God knows best – that God commanded us to know Him and turned us over to ourselves in gaining this knowledge only because He knew that we do not perceive and we do not know the reality of ourselves and that we are incapable of knowing ourselves. Hence we come to know that we are even more incapable of knowing Him. This is know-ledge of Him/not knowledge.[3]

Prophetic knowledge

For Muslims, one of the more convincing proofs that people do not and cannot know themselves is the fact that God sent prophets. If people could know themselves, they could discover on their own what is good for them and bad for them. But in fact, they are not even sure what is good and bad for their bodies, much less their whole selves. And I do not mean only ordinary people, I mean all the great experts, like the medical doctors, who change their opinions about what is good and bad for us on a fairly regular basis.

The function of the prophets is to tell people what is good and bad for the whole self. The self has no end, even if it does have a beginning. Prophetic instructions deal with the self in terms of its endlessness. From this standpoint, physical death is rather insignificant, though it does mark an important boundary.

After death, people will no longer have the freedom to choose or reject God's guidance. They will simply serve God in the way He wants them to serve Him, because they will no longer be able to hide in their ignorance, which is to say that they will no longer be able to "bury" the self in heedlessness.

The guidance brought by the prophets tells people not so much who they are as who they are not. They are *not* beings with limited, finite, finished identities, and they can never, ever be such beings. If they could reach a final limit, they would either be no different from God, which is impossible, or they would come to a grinding halt in their experience of the Real, which is also impossible. In fact, they live today and they will live forever in the process of change. They cannot, by themselves, see much beyond today, certainly not beyond death. The prophetic knowledge tells them what is good and bad for the self – this self that has no end and no specific identity.

The prophetic knowledge tells people that *tazkiyat an-nafs* is good for them and that they should pursue it. They need to cultivate the self. This is both purification of the self, or turning it away from everything that is bad for it, and augmentation of the self, or gaining everything that is good for it. In other words, cultivating the self is to provide for its well-being, and this needs to be defined in terms of everlasting existence and endless trans-formation. Since, on their own and without God's help, people have no possible way of knowing what the afterlife is all about, they have no possible way of knowing what will have a good or bad effect upon their becoming in the next world. It is the role of the prophetic messages to provide this knowledge. The fundamental insight here is that we do not know and cannot possibly know who we are on our own. Only the Creator of the self can provide the knowledge that allows for taking care of the self in a way that will guarantee its permanent well-being.

From the standpoint of the Sufi tradition, there is nothing more damaging to the well-being of the self than the notion that we know who we are and that we do not need help, or only a little bit of help, or only the help of the imagined "experts," to put our affairs in order. In the Sufi reading, this notion of not needing prophetic help is the fatal defect of the modern world. Modern science, technology, and all the other branches of learning – not to speak of politics – are nothing but ignorance of the self masquerading as knowledge. Attempts to rationalize the world and to use it for our own benefit are doomed to failure, because we cannot possibly know where our benefit lies. This is the ultimate folly of "self-help." The only way we can pretend to know our selves in order to help our selves is to bury our selves in false knowledge, pretending to know what we do not and cannot know. People do this by defining the self in limited terms – biological terms, anthropological terms, psychological terms, historical terms, economic terms, social terms, ideological terms, theological terms, Islamist terms. These failed attempts to understand the self go a long way toward explaining the historically unprecedented blood-letting of the twentieth century.

Finally, let me return once more to the Koranic passage that I cited at the beginning of the chapter, though I translate it a bit differently: "By the self and That which proportioned it, and inspired it to its depravity and its godwariness. Prosperous is he who cultivates it, and failed has he who buries it." In short, these verses mean that God has created people and given them everything that they are. But what they are can never fully be known, because what God gives them has no end. Part of what He gives is knowledge through the prophets. Its function is to specify "depravity," which turns people away from God and their own true nature, and "godwariness," which brings about prosperity and well-being. Those who cultivate their selves by following the prophetic instructions will achieve the everlasting wholeness and well-being of the self, but those who bury their selves in ignorance and forgetfulness will have wronged no one but themselves.

5

The remembrance of God

The Koran commonly refers to the knowledge brought by the prophets as "remembrance" (*dhikr*) and "reminder" (*dhikra, tadhkir*), terms that derive from the root *dh-k-r*. The Koran calls itself by these words more than forty times, and it refers to other prophetic messages, like the Torah and the Gospel, by the same words. The basic Koranic understanding of the necessity for a plurality of prophets is that Adam's children kept on falling into heedlessness and forgetfulness, which is the shortcoming of their father. The only cure for this shortcoming is the remembrance that God provides by means of the prophets.

If the Koran is a "remembrance," so also is the human response to it. To be truly human is to remember – to acknowledge and confirm what we already know. "Not equal are the blind and the seeing, those who have faith and do wholesome deeds and the ugly-doer. Little do you remember!" (40:58). What needs to be remembered is the Trust, which human beings have accepted to carry by the very fact of being human. In other terms, what needs to be remembered is the truth, the reality, the real (*haqq*), which is nothing but the plain fact of God's activity and presence in the world and the soul. To remember God in His activity and presence is to remember Him as He is, and this is to see that there is nothing truly real but the Real.

It was mentioned that the Sufis use this same word *dhikr* to designate the method of achieving one-pointed concentration on their Beloved. More than anything else, it is this practice that differentiates Sufi Muslims from non-Sufi Muslims. The word means not only to remember, but also to mention. Because the Sufi practice of *dhikr* can be described as a type of incantatory prayer, the word is often translated as "invocation." In its most basic forms, it involves the repetition of a name or names of God, often embedded in set phrases such as "Praise belongs to God."

The sources frequently discuss *dhikr* in conjunction with *du'a'* or supplication, which literally means "calling (upon God)." *Du'a'* differs from *dhikr* because it usually takes the form of a request, does not employ set formulas, and is not repetitive. Any petitionary prayer in any language can be called a "supplication," whereas *dhikr* employs Arabic names and formulas drawn from the Koran or the Hadith. Both remembrance and supplication are voluntary acts, and they need to be distinguished from the daily prayer (*salat*), which is required from all the faithful.

Studies of *dhikr* in Western languages have usually emphasized various techniques that Sufis employ in achieving concentration. Focusing on technique obscures the centrality of *dhikr* in the Koran, where the term is employed, along with closely related derivatives, about 270 times. Despite the Western fascination with techniques, these have always been of secondary interest within the Sufi tradition itself. Nor is it necessary to search for outside influence to explain their genesis. Perseverance in remembering God – and sincere Islam is nothing if not this – will eventually entail a certain concern with the technical aspects of controlling one's thoughts and focusing one's attention, and this cannot ignore posture and breathing.[1]

The basic meaning of the term *dhikr* can be brought out by answering three questions – what, why, and how. What is to be remembered? Why should it be remembered? How can it be remembered? The object of remembrance is God, whose reality is designated briefly by the first Shahadah, "There is no god but God," and in more detail by the whole range of names and attributes mentioned in the Koran. This object *should* be remembered because He has commanded human beings to remember Him and because ultimate happiness depends upon remembrance. The object *can* be remembered by imitating the Prophet, whose Sunnah provides the model for right activity and right remembrance.

In short, to understand the full implications of the term *dhikr* in the Koran and the tradition, one needs to have a clear understanding of the remembered object. To understand God Islamically, one needs to grasp how He reveals Himself through the Koran. This means that *dhikr* brings up three basic topics – God, His self-revelation, and the implications of this self-revelation for human beings. These three are summarized as the principles of faith – *tawhid,* prophecy, and the return to God. The last needs to be considered in its widest sense, embracing both the "compulsory return" through death and the "voluntary return" through following the Prophet.

Dhikr in the Koran and Hadith

The Koran employs the term *dhikr Allah,* "the remembrance of God," twenty-six times in nominal or verbal form. In several other instances, the word *ism* ("name") is inserted in the middle of this phrase, thereby emphasizing the verbal mention of God's name. For example, people are commanded to remember – that is, mention – God's name before sacrificing animals (5:4, 6:118, and elsewhere). However, the command to mention God's name is also a general one, as seen in verses like this: "And remember the name of your Lord, and devote yourself to Him" (73:8); "And remember the name of your Lord, morning and evening" (76:25).

These Koranic verses help explain why the expression "remembrance of God" is normally interpreted as requiring the mention of His name, even if "name" is not part of the phrase. As a practice, *dhikr* demands an articulation of the divine in the form of one of His revealed names, whether this occurs vocally or mentally. *Dhikr* has never been understood as a vague or general recollection of God's presence or activity.

The central importance in the Koran of remembering God becomes clear as soon as we notice that the book commands few acts as vigorously. Fifteen verses command people to remember God. But obedience to such commands is not the only imperative that drives people to perform *dhikr*. A second imperative pertains to the human situation as framed in Islamic terms. People must remember God because true life – life with God in the next world – depends upon it. In Koranic language, "to be forgotten by God" is to burn in the Fire, and to be remembered by God is to dwell in the Garden. Speaking of the resurrection, God says, "Today We forget you, even as you forgot the encounter of this your day; and your refuge is the Fire" (45:34). Such verses help explain why Ibn Ata'illah Iskandari (d. 1309) can say, in his well-known treatise on *dhikr,* "All acts of worship will disappear from the servant on the Day of Mustering, except the remembrance of God, asserting unity [*tawhid*], and praise [of Him]."[2]

Just as *dhikr* brings about happiness in the next world, so too it provides the way to achieve nearness to God in this world. The hearts of the unbelievers, in contrast to the hearts of the godwary, are "hardened against the remembrance of God" (39:22). Note the emphasis through repetition in this verse: "Those who have faith, their hearts being at peace in God's remembrance – in God's remembrance are at peace the hearts of those who have faith and do wholesome deeds; theirs is blessedness and a fair resort" (13:28).

In short, to achieve a heart at peace in this world and the next, one needs to remember God, for it calls down God's response. The verse "Remember Me, and I will remember you" (2:152) provides a specific practice that is only implied in the verse "Say: If you love God, follow me, and God will love you'" (3:31). One of the Prophet's names is Dhikr Allah, and following him is to remember God. "You have a good example in God's Messenger, for whosoever hopes for God and the Last Day and remembers God frequently" (33:21). The Sunnah provides the details of how to remember God in every act of life. In his treatise on *dhikr,* Ibn Ata'illah quotes a hadith that illustrates the intimate link that Muslims have always seen between love for God and the Prophet and remembering God and the Prophet:

> God said to him, "O Muhammad, I have made you one of the remembrances of Me. Those who remember you remember Me, and those who love you love Me." Hence the Prophet said, "Those who remember me have remembered God, and those who love me have loved God."[3]

The Hadith literature provides a wealth of material that corroborates the Koranic picture and emphasizes the benefits of *dhikr* beyond the grave. The Prophet calls *dhikr* the best act of worship. Every word a person utters in this life will be counted against him or her in the next life, except bidding to honor (*amr bi'l-ma'ruf*), forbidding dishonor (*nahy an al-munkar*), and remembering God. When someone complained about Islam's many commands and prohibitions and asked for a single practice to which he could cling, the Prophet replied, "Let your tongue stay moist with the remembrance of God." He reported that God says, "I am with My servant when he remembers Me. If he remembers Me in himself, I remember him in Myself, and if he remembers Me in an assembly, I remember him in an assembly better than his." Such "assemblies" of God's remembrance are well attested in the Prophet's time, and they become the model for Sun gatherings.

The hadiths make clear that the important formulas of remembrance are those still heard throughout the Islamic world on every sort of occasion – "No god but God," "Praise belongs to God," "Glory be to God," "God is greater," and "There is no power and no strength but in God." All but the last are found word for word in the Koran.

The hadiths also make clear that all of God's names, traditionally said to number ninety-nine, may be employed in remembrance and supplication. The implication is that each name of God has a specific characteristic that is conveyed to those who remember it. Many hadiths allude to "the greatest name of God" (*al-ism al-a'zam*), which is "the name by which, when God is called. He answers, and when asked. He gives." Litanies (*awrad, ahzab*) composed of divine names, formulas of remembrance, and Koranic verses have been common among Muslims from earliest times, and they became a hallmark of Sufi practice, second only to *dhikr*. Some of them mention the ninety-nine most beautiful names. One of them, the "Great Coat of Mail" (*al-jawshan al-kabir*), illustrates the enormous richness of the Arabic language by employing one thousand names of God.[4]

Dhikr in the Sufi tradition

Given the centrality of God's remembrance in the Koran and Hadith, there can be no question that *dhikr* was basic to Islamic practice throughout the early centuries. As the jurists gradually codified the Sharia, however, they could not impose *dhikr* on the community. Even though the Koran repeatedly commands people to remember God, by nature *dhikr* is connected much more to intention and awareness than to the outward activity that is ruled by the Sharia. Nonetheless, given the broad sense in which the term is used in the Koran, it was not stepping outside the Koranic meaning to say that reciting the Koran, the "Remembrance" par excellence, is nothing but the practice of remembering God. Moreover, the Koran makes clear that the daily prayer (*salat*) is itself remembrance of God. In these senses of the word, the jurists did make *dhikr* incumbent on all Muslims. Moreover, they wrote voluminously on supplications and formulas of remembrance with which all Muslims should occupy themselves as much as possible. But, for the Sharia, these practices can only be considered recommended and praise-worthy, not incumbent and mandatory.

The Sufis are distinguished from other Muslims partly because they consider the remembrance of God, in the form of mentioning His names as instructed by their shaykhs, as incumbent, not merely recommended. It is they who constantly remind us that the essence of all the ritual activities, after all, is remembering God. Why should people pray and fast? To remember God, to keep Him constantly in mind. "*Ihsan* is to worship God as if you see Him," and keeping the tongue moist with the mention of His name is an aid in doing this. The Naqshbandi shaykh Khwaja Muhammad Parsa (d. 1420) writes, "The root of being a Muslim is 'No god but God,' words that are identical with remembrance." Hence, he says, the spirit of the daily prayer and the other ritual practices, such as fasting and pilgrimage, is "the renewal of God's remembrance in the heart."[5]

In the same way, the Sufis considered all Islamic theoretical teachings to be aimed at awakening remembrance in the soul. In commenting on the Koranic teachings, they demonstrate that *dhikr* implies far more than just the ritual activities that go by the name. Full remembrance means actualizing all the perfections latent in the original human disposition (*fitra*) by virtue of its being a divine image. Ghazali and many others speak of human perfection as "assuming the traits of the divine names" (*al-takhal-luq bi'l-asma' al-ilahiyya*). The name *Allah* is the all-comprehensive name (*al-ism al-jami'*), or the referent of all the other divine names, so the stage of full human perfection is sometimes called "being like unto Allah" (*ta'alluh*), which might also be translated as "deiformity" or "theomorphism." For many of the Sufis, the remembrance of the name Allah itself is the sign of the fully realized human individual to whom reference is made in the prophetic saying, "The Last Hour will not come as long as there remains anyone in this world saying, 'God, God!'"[6]

The hallmark of the divine image in which human beings were created is the intelligence that sets them apart from all other creatures. Turning to God – remembrance – awakens awareness of God in the heart and actualizes the divine image latent in the soul. Ultimate felicity is nothing but the remembrance of the wellspring of our own true nature, and that is God Himself; or, it is the realization of genuine human character traits, which are the traces of God's names.

The Shahadah is commonly called "the best *dhikr*." As we have seen, it encapsulates all Sufi teachings and practices. The goal in remembering God is to annihilate everything other than God and to come to subsist in the divine. As Ibn Ata'illah puts it, "No one says No *god but God* correctly unless he negates everything other than God from his soul and heart."[7] His contemporary Najm ad-Din Razi writes,

> With *no god* the practitioner negates other than the Real, and with *but God* he affirms the Presence of Exaltation. When he does this constantly and clings to it, the spirit's attachment to other than God is gradually cut with the scissors of *no god*. The beauty of *but God's* authority discloses itself from behind the Pavilion of Exaltation. In keeping with the promise, *Remember Me, and I will remember you* [2:152], the remembrance is disengaged from the clothing of letters and sound. The specific characteristics of *Everything is perishing but His face* [28:88] become evident in the disclosure of the light of Divinity's magnificence.[8]

Although many authorities agree that "No god but God" is the most excellent formula of remembrance, others hold that the "single remembrance" (*al-dhikr al-mufrad*) – the mention of the name Allah alone – is superior. Ibn Arabi often quotes approvingly the words of one of his masters, Abu'l-Abbas Uryabi, who held that the single name is best, because in remembering "No god but God," one might die in the frightful distance of negation, but in remembering God alone, one can only die in the intimacy of affirmation.[9]

Sufi masters employed specific names and formulas of remembrance to bring out the spiritual potentialities and mold the character traits of their disciples. Many Sufi works provide information on names that can be appropriately used – though never without the permission and inculcation (*talqin*) of a master – by disciples at different stages of spiritual growth. Works on the "most beautiful names," such as Ghazali's *al-Maqsad al-asna* ("The Highest Goal"),[10] often discuss the moral traits and spiritual attitudes that reflect each of the individual names on the human level. Ibn Ata'illah devotes several pages to the properties of various names and their influence on seekers at different stages of the path. He points out, for example, that the name Wealthy or Independent (*al-ghani*) *is* useful for those who seek disengagement (*tajrid*) from phenomena but are unable to achieve it. The name Bestower of Favors (*al-mannan*) is beneficial to those who have passed beyond the enjoyments of the lower self, but harmful for those who still have egocentric needs.[11]

Despite the many discussions of the benefits of specific names, the texts frequently state that those who remember God's names should not be concerned with immediate or deferred benefits and goals. Rather, they should exemplify the attitude expressed in the prayer of Rabi'a: "O God, if I worship You for fear of hell, burn me in hell, and if I worship You in hope of paradise, forbid it to me. But if I worship You for You, do not hold back from me the Everlasting Beauty."[12]

Some Sufis spoke of transcending *dhikr,* since in the last analysis remembering God is an attribute of the seeker and therefore pertains to the domain of other than God. According to an-Nuri (d. 907), true remembrance is "the annihilation of the rememberer in the Remembered."[13] Ibn Arabi explains that there can be no remembrance after the veil has been lifted, for when the traveler "witnesses" (mushahada) God, the individual self is annihilated.

> There is no remembrance along with witnessing. Hence the rememberers must be veiled. Although [a hadith says] "God sits with those who remember Him," this is from behind the veil of remembrance. Whenever someone's object of seeking is behind a veil, he cannot be at ease. When the veil is lifted, witnessing occurs, and the remembrance disappears in the self-disclosure of the Remembered.[14]

Ibn Arabi's disciple Qunawi (d. 1274) writes that the traveler must gradually abandon all remembrance, both outward and inward, until total emptiness is achieved.[15] Nonetheless, the final word for most seekers remains with Ibn Arabi: "Remembrance is more excellent than abandoning it, for one can only abandon it during witnessing, and witnessing cannot be achieved in an absolute sense."[16]

Many classifications of dhikr can be found in Sufi works. Some of these refer to the depth of concentration achieved by the disciple, such as remembrance of the tongue, of the heart, and of the inmost mystery or secret heart (sirr). Another common distinction is that between loud or public and silent or private dhikr. The loud dhikr was usually performed in groups according to various ritual forms that took shape in the different Sufi orders. Sessions of public invocation range from the reserved to the ecstatic. Some groups, such as the Mawlawiyya (which looks back to Rumi as its founder), considered music and dance as aids to concentration. Other groups banned anything but Koranic recitation and group recital of names and formulas. Most Sufis would probably agree that group sessions are a secondary form of Sufi practice, since the seeker's progress on the path, to the extent that it does not derive totally from God's grace, depends upon individual efforts. Sa'di (d. 1292) is not speaking metaphorically when he says at the beginning of his famous *Gulistan*, "Every breath taken in replenishes life, and once let go it gives joy to the soul. So each breath counts as two blessings, and each blessing requires thanksgiving." It is the silent and persevering remembrance of God in gratitude for each breath or each heartbeat, always within the context of the Sunnah, that takes the seeker to the ultimate goal.

6
The way of love

From about the thirteenth century onward, few themes play as important a role in Sufi teachings as love. Historians have commonly spoken of a gradual development of Sufism that begins in a mysticism of asceticism and fear, slowly changes to an emphasis on love and devotion, and then turns to stressing knowledge and gnosis. Some have suggested that these three ways of approaching God correspond with the three basic Hindu paths – karma yoga, bhakti yoga, and jnana yoga. Whatever the heuristic value of such schemes, there can be no doubt that from earliest times Muslims who strove to gain nearness to God did so through activity, love, and knowledge. Any close reading of the Koran will make clear that it prefigures the diverse possibilities of the soul's unfolding. And any close reading of Sufi literature will reveal sophisticated insights into the soul's complexity at every period.

It might be argued that Islam is built on karma yoga, since everyone without exception must observe the Sharia, which sets down the path of conforming to God's will through activity. One can also argue that Muslims and Sufis stress jnana yoga, because, generally speaking, they place a higher value on knowledge than do Jews or Christians. Nonetheless, Sufism gives a certain pride of place to love. In what follows, I want to make a few brief suggestions as to the significance of love as expressed in the two great watersheds of the tradition, Rumi and Ibn Arabi. I do not wish to suggest that either neglected the paths of knowledge and activity, and indeed, in the case of Ibn Arabi, a strong argument can be made that he gave priority to knowledge. Rather, I simply want to bring out the basic Sufi understanding of love's reality, given that love is so often the central concern of the texts.

Although love is rarely emphasized in the earliest expressions of Sufism, the Koran speaks of love in a number of key verses that clarify its essential role. We have already discussed one of these verses, which tells us that God's love for people grows up in keeping with their success in conforming themselves to the Prophet's example. Although this verse speaks of love for God as a precondition for receiving God's love in return, all the great lovers recognized that what stirs up love for God in the first place is God's love for human beings. People could not love God if He did not already love them. The Hadith of the Hidden Treasure makes precisely this point – God created people out of love for them. The most often cited Koranic proof text for this hierarchy of love is the verse, "He loves them, and they love Him" (5:54). First God loves human beings, then human beings love God. Once they come to love Him, His love for them will increase to the extent that they follow the Prophet, purify and cultivate their souls, remember God ceaselessly, and become perfect human beings.

Whether or not love is mentioned, the earliest expressions of Sufism's reality tend to take the form of pithy sayings touching on a great variety of topics having to do with the path to God. Two or three figures appear who are looked back upon as exemplars of the life of love, like Rabi'a and Hallaj. But from the eleventh to the thirteenth centuries – the fifth to the seventh Islamic centuries – a number of extremely important authors appear who map out a detailed psychology of love. The famous Ghazali sometimes writes about human and divine love, but his less well-known brother, Ahmad Ghazali (d. 1126), devotes most of his relatively short Persian work, *Sawanih,* to love as the underlying, unitive reality of the soul. This work then provides inspiration for dozens of later treatises. Ahmad's disciple Ayn al-Qudat Hamadani (d. 1131) played an important role in formulating a psychology and metaphysics of love. Perhaps most profound and original in approach – in a period of many great masters – was Ahmad Sam'ani (d. 1140), even though he has remained almost completely unknown to modern scholars. (More will be said about him in chapter 9). Somewhat later appeared the great Persian poet Attar (d. 1221), whose works mapped out all the themes of love.

Despite the large number of authors who wrote on divine and human love, Ibn Arabi and Rumi can be considered the two greatest masters of the tradition. Ibn Arabi was born in Murcia in Spain and died in Damascus in 1240. He wrote prolifically in Arabic and came to be considered the foremost Sufi theologian and philosopher. In later centuries, his name became almost synonymous with the expression *wahdat al-wujud,* "the Unity of Being," a doctrine that was often taken as encapsulating his perspective.[1] He composed more than five hundred prose works, some of them enormously long. He also wrote something like twenty thousand verses of poetry. His younger contemporary, Rumi, was born in Baikh in present-day Afghanistan and moved in his youth to Anatolia, eventually settling in Konya in present-day Turkey, where he died in 1273. He composed about sixty-five thousand verses of breathtaking Persian poetry along with three short prose works. The Persianate world, from Turkey to India, looks back upon Rumi as the greatest spiritual poet of history, just as the whole Islamic world considers Ibn Arabi the greatest Sufi theoretician.

Ibn Arabi and Rumi belong to two different strands of Sufism. Each in his own way marks the high point of the tradition. Most formulations of Sufi teachings after them are inspired to some degree by the writings of one or both. Their perspectives differed in many ways, but they also share numerous common themes, especially on the issue of love. In what follows, I will illustrate how Ibn Arabi explains something of love's reality and offer a few appropriate examples of Rumi's poetical expressions of the same ideas.

Love's creativity

Love cannot be defined, though its traces can be described. On this point Ibn Arabi the theoretician and Rumi the poet agree completely:

> Love has no definition through which its essence can be known. Rather, it is given descriptive and verbal definitions, nothing more. Those who define love have not known it, those who have not tasted it by drinking it down have not known it, and those who say that they have been quenched by it have not known it, for love is drinking without quenching.[2]

★

> Someone asked, "What is loverhood?"
>   I replied, "Don't ask me about these meanings –
> "When you become like me, you'll know;
>   When it calls you, you'll tell its tale."[3]

★

> What is it to be a lover? To have perfect thirst.
>   So let me explain the water of life.[4]

On the divine level, love can be called the motive force for God's creative activity. In one of his many commentaries on the Hadith of the Hidden Treasure, Ibn Arabi tells us that the kind of knowledge that God loved to achieve through creation was a knowledge that had its origin in time, since He already knew Himself and all things in eternity. Ibn Arabi makes this remark while drawing a parallel between sexual union for the purpose of having children and God's love to be known for the purpose of creating the universe.

> When the marriage union occurs because of the love for reproduction and procreation, it joins the divine love when there was no cosmos. He "loved to be known." So, because of this love, He turned His desire toward the things while they were

in the state of nonexistence. They were standing in the station
of the root because of the preparedness of their own possibility.
He said to them, *Be!*, so they came to be, that He might be
known by every sort of knowledge. This was temporal knowledge. As yet it had no object, because the one who knows by
it was not yet qualified by existence. His love sought the
perfection of knowledge and the perfection of existence.[5]

In another passage, Ibn Arabi explains the meaning of God's
love to be known while commenting on the Koranic verse,
"And He is with you wherever you are" (57:4). God's love
for human beings means that He never lets them out of His
sight.

God's love for His servants is not qualified by origin or end, for
it does not accept qualities that are temporal or accidental . . .
Hence the relation of God's love to them is the same as the fact
that *He is with* them *wherever* they *are* [57:4] . . . Just as He is
with them in the state of their existence, so also He is with
them in the state of their nonexistence, for they are the objects
of His knowledge. He witnesses them and loves them never-
endingly . . . He has always loved His creatures, just as He has
always known them . . . His existence has no first point, so His
love for His servants has no first point.[6]

In one of his prose works, Rumi explains the significance of the
Hidden Treasure by referring to the two categories of God's
attributes – mercy and wrath, or gentleness and severity. God
created the world to make all his attributes manifest, and this
demands infinite diversity:

God says, "I was a hidden treasure, so I loved to be known."
In other words, "I created the whole cosmos, and the goal in
all of it was to make Myself manifest, sometimes through
gentleness and sometimes through severity." God is not the sort
of king for whom a single herald would be sufficient. Were all

the atoms of the universe His heralds, they would fall short and be incapable of making Him known.[7]

Rumi frequently points to love as God's motive for creation by commenting on a divine saying addressed to Muhammad: "But for you, I would not have created the heavenly spheres." The Prophet is the fullness of realized love, through whom and for whom the universe was created.

Love makes the ocean boil like a pot,
  love grinds mountains down to sand.
Love splits the heaven in a hundred pieces,
  love shakes the earth with a mighty shaking.
Pure love was paired with Muhammad –
  because of love God said to him, "But for you."
Since he alone was the goal of love,
  he was singled out from all the prophets.
"If not for pure love,
  why would I give existence to the spheres?
"I raised the celestial wheel on high
  so that you might understand love's elevation."[8]

The true beloved

God created the world through love, so love produces the multiplicity that fills the universe. He never ceases loving the creatures, so He never ceases creating them, and this keeps the universe in a perpetual state of transformation and flux. All things are infused with love, because God's attribute of love brings them into existence and motivates all their activities.

The Prophet said, "God is beautiful and He loves beauty" and this is an established hadith. So, He described Himself as loving beauty, and He loves the cosmos. Hence, there is nothing more beautiful than the cosmos. And He is beautiful, while beauty is intrinsically lovable, so the whole cosmos loves God. The beauty of His artisanry permeates His creation, while the cosmos is the loci wherein He becomes manifest. Therefore the love of some parts of the cosmos for other parts derives from God's love for Himself.[9]

*

God's wisdom through His destiny and decree
  made us lovers one of another.
That foreordainment paired all the world's parts
  and set each in love with its mate . . .
The female inclines towards the male
  so that each may perfect the other's work.
God placed inclination in man and woman
  so the world may subsist through their union.[10]

Love's creative power does not stop at the externalization and maintenance of the cosmos. Although the jewels of the Hidden Treasure have been thrown out into the open, most creatures do not recognize them for what they are, nor do they understand that their own loves and desires externalize God's love. Their love is simply God's own love reflected in the creatures. It follows that, as Ibn Arabi puts it, "None loves God but God,"[11] and "There is no lover and no beloved but God."[12] Lovers grasp this when they reach the point of seeing God in everything that exists. This is the fully realized love mentioned in the hadith, "When I love My servant, I am his hearing through which he hears, his sight through which he sees." Ibn Arabi writes,

The soul sees that it sees Him only through Him, not through itself, and that it loves Him only through Him, not through itself. So He it is who loves Himself – it is not the soul that loves Him. The soul gazes upon Him in every existent by means of His very eye. Hence it knows that none loves Him but He. He is the lover and the beloved, the seeker and the sought.[13]

Rumi provides many parallel accounts of God's love that courses through all things. But his perspective focuses more on practice than theory, so he constantly reminds his readers of their own situation. Here is one of his ghazals:

> It is incumbent on lovers to seek the Friend,
>   flowing like floods on face and head to His river.
> He himself does the seeking, and we are like shadows.
>   All our talking and speaking are the words of the Friend.
> Sometimes we rejoice like water running in His stream,
>   sometimes we're trapped like water in His jug.
> Again we boil like carrots in a pot while He stirs
>   with the ladle of thought – such is the Friend's temper.
> He puts His mouth to our ear and whispers
>   and our soul quickly takes on His fragrance.
> He comes like the spirit's spirit, leaving no escape –
>   never have I seen a spirit that was an enemy of the Friend!
> He will melt you with coquetry, making you frail as a hair –
>   but you would not take the two worlds for a hair of the Friend.
> We sit with the Friend saying, "Friend, where [ku] are you?"
>   Drunk, we keep on cooing [ku] in the lane of the Friend.
> Unhappy pictures and ugly thoughts
>   come from an idle nature – not from the Friend.
> Be silent, so that He Himself may describe Himself!
>   What does your cold "hey, hey" have to do with His "hey, hey"?![14]

Ibn Arabi and especially Rumi constantly remind their readers that love for any creature can only be love for God. Only ignorance veils people from perceiving what they love. Ibn Arabi writes,

> None but God is loved in the existent things. It is He who is manifest within every beloved to the eye of every lover – and there is no existent thing that is not a lover. So, the cosmos is

all lover and beloved, and all of it goes back to Him. In the same way, no one is worshiped but Him, for no worshiper worships anything without imagining divinity within it. Otherwise, he would not worship it. Thus God says, *Your Lord has decreed that you worship none but Him* [17:23].

So also is love. No one loves anyone but his own Creator, but he is veiled from Him by love for Zaynab, Su'ad, Hind, Layla, this world, money, position, and everything loved in the world. Poets exhaust their words on all these existing things, but they do not know. The gnostics never hear a verse, a riddle, a panegyric, or a love poem that is not about God, hidden beyond the veil of forms.[15]

In his major prose work, Rumi makes the same point with these words:

All the hopes, desires, loves, and affections that people have for different things – father, mother, friends, heavens, earth, gardens, palaces, sciences, deeds, food, drink – all these are desires for God, and these things are veils. When people leave this world and see the Eternal King without these veils, then they will know that all these were veils and coverings and that the object of their desire was in reality that One Thing. All their difficulties will be solved, all the questions and perplexities that they had in their hearts will be answered, and they will see all things face to face.[16]

All love is in truth love for God. Love is good because it is divine, but it remains a deceptive veil so long as lovers do not recognize its true object.

Love is an attribute of God, who has no needs –
     love for anything else is a metaphor.
The beauty of the others is gold-plated:
     outwardly it is light, inwardly smoke
When the light goes and the smoke appears,
     metaphorical love turns to ice.

The beauty returns to its own root,
  the body is left – putrid, disgraced, ugly.
The moonlight goes back to the moon,
  the moon's reflection leaves the wall.
Water and clay remain with no picture –
  without the moon, the wall becomes fiendish.
When gold jumps from the face of counterfeit coin,
  it returns to sit in its own mine.
The disgraced copper stays like smoke –
  and even more ashamed is its lover.
Those with eyes turn their love to the mine of gold,
  each day their love increasing.
The mine has no partner in its goldness –
  hail, O Mine of Gold! In You there is no doubt.[17]

Love is an ever-present reality, but it tends to be dispersed and dissipated because people fall in love with the Beloved's reflections. Here we come back to the centrality of knowledge. Even though Rumi devotes all his works to love, he frequently reminds us that true love depends upon discernment. The lover must be able to distinguish gold from gold-plate.

Love makes bitter sweet,
  love turns copper to gold,
Love makes dregs into wine,
  love turns pain into healing,
Love brings the dead to life,
  love makes kings into slaves –
But this love results from knowledge.
  When did a fool sit on this throne?
How can faulty knowledge give birth to love?
  It gives birth to love, but love for inanimate things.
When it sees the color of its desire in the things,
  it hears the call of the beloved in a whistle.

> Faulty knowledge does not know the difference –
> it thinks that lightning is the sun.[18]

In short, love for God grows up from the basic declaration of faith, the assertion of God's unique reality – "No god but God." Since love is a divine attribute, it follows that "There is no true lover and no true beloved but God." Once the lovers see things clearly, they find that they love everything in creation, because all of creation displays God's beauty, and their own love displays God's love. Ibn Arabi tells us that when the seekers pass beyond "natural" and "spiritual" love, they reach the stage of "divine" love, where they love God in all things through God's own love of the things. Then they love all things in every dimension of existence.

> The mark of divine love is love for all beings in every domain
> – spiritual, sensory, imaginal, and imaginary. Every domain has
> an eye that it receives from His name Light, an eye with which
> it looks upon His name Beautiful.[19]

When their love is complete, the lovers live in the joy of experiencing their own union with the One who is both lover and beloved. As Rumi puts it,

> The joy and heartache of lovers is He,
> the wages and salary for service is He.
> If they were to gaze on other than the Beloved,
> how could that be love? That would be idle fancy.
> Love is that flame which, when it blazes up,
> burns away all except the everlasting Beloved.
> It slays "other than God" with the sword of *no god*.
> Look carefully: After *no god* what remains?
> There remains *but God,* the rest has gone.
> Hail, O Love, great burner of all others!
> It is He alone who is first and last,
> all else grows up from the eye that sees double.[20]

The religion of love

The precondition for love is the ability to see straight. This demands that we understand our own inadequacies and limitations. We must acknowledge that we do not know who we are. Knowing our own ignorance and inadequacy, we know that God alone is adequate. We are far from the Real, far from wholeness, far from balance, equilibrium, wisdom, compassion, and every other desirable quality. Truly understanding and savoring this inadequacy yields a deep longing in the soul, which Rumi commonly calls "pain."

> Whoever is more awake has greater pain,
> whoever is more aware has a paler face.[21]

Dwelling on one's pain and imperfection can only call down the remedy. Rumi frequently urges his readers to seek out pain and suffering, to become thirsty and not to look for water.

> Since the world's Remedy is searching
> for pain and disease,
> we have cut ourselves off from remedies
> and are the companions of pain.[22]

The knowledge of human inadequacy is knowledge of our essential nothingness. The Koran sometimes calls this human nothingness "poverty" (faqr), a word which, in Islamic languages, is a far more common designation for what we have been calling "Sufism" than the word tasawwuf itself. Both fakir (Arabic faqir) and dervish (Persian darwish) mean "poor man," that is, a traveler on the Sufi path. The term is taken from the Koran, especially the verse, "O people, you are the poor toward God; and God – He is the Wealthy, the Praiseworthy" (35:15). As Ibn Arabi says, "Poverty is an affair that is inherent in everything other than God. There is no way to escape from it."[23] Rumi writes,

> Poverty is not for the sake of hardship –
>   no, it is because nothing exists but God.[24]

Sufism is poverty toward God. To be poor toward Him is to acknowledge one's need for Him, and the deeper and more sincere this acknowledgment becomes, the more it turns into an overpowering drive to reach the Beloved. Few pains are as deep as the lovers' pain in their separation. Knowing their own pain, the lovers yearn for the cure of every pain, and that is their Beloved. The end result is deliverance from pain and union with all joy, but without pain, the journey will never begin.

> First You empty the lovers at the hand of separation,
>   then You fill them with gold to the tops of their heads![25]

Rumi has thousands of verses on the interplay between separation and union, hope and fear, sobriety and drunkenness, annihilation and subsistence, pain and joy. This is the dialectic of love. No love is possible without the ups and downs inherent to the created realm. He constantly invites his readers to leap into the fray. This ghazal is typical:

> How much the Companion made me suffer until this work
>   settled into the eye's water and the liver's blood!
> A thousand fires and smokes and heartaches all named
>   "Love"!
> A thousand pains and regrets and afflictions all named
>   "Companion"!
> If you are the enemy of your own self, come – in the name
>   of God!
> Welcome to the soul's sacrifice! Welcome to a pitiful slaughter!
> Look at me – I see Him worth a hundred deaths like this.
>   I neither fear nor flee from the Heart-keeper's slaying.
> Like the Nile's water, love's torture has two faces –
>   water for its own folk, blood-drinking for others.

If aloes and candles didn't burn, what good would they be?
  Aloes would be the same as the trunk of a thornbush.
If battles had no striking of swords and spears and arrows,
  how would a catamite be different from Rustam the hero?
Rustam finds the sword sweeter than sugar,
  he sees the arrows raining down better than coins of gold.
This lion takes her prey with two hundred coquetries –
  the prey runs in desire for her wave after wave.
The slain prey keeps on screaming in the midst of the blood –
  "For God's sake, kill me again!"
The eyes of the slain gaze at the living –
  "O heedless and frozen, come, don't scratch your heads!"
Silence, silence! Love's allusions are upside-down –
  too much speaking keeps the meanings hidden.[26]

If Rumi objects to his own poetical expressions of love, all the more would he object to the attempts by Ibn Arabi and other theoretically minded Sufis to explain love's reality. Love needs to be tasted and experienced, and poetry is far more adequate than rational disquisition to expressing experience. In place of offering more of Ibn Arabi's explanations, I present three of Rumi's ghazals, without any attempt to clarify the images and allusions. Nor will I try to explain why the poems need to be read as references to the divine Beloved rather than a human beloved (the ambiguity is increased in Persian because pronouns have no gender and capital letters are not employed). For lovers, the issue does not arise. As Ibn Arabi puts it in a passage already quoted, "The gnostics never hear a verse, a riddle, a panegyric, or a love poem that is not about God, hidden beyond the veil of forms."

If someone falls in love with that splendor of the meadow,
  don't wonder that he's lost his heart in love like me.
Don't speak of patience – patience will never find its way
  to the heart that has been tested by that Friend.

When love rattles intellect's chain,
   Plato and Avicenna go mad.
By the spirit of love! No spirit escapes love –
   even within a hundred fortresses, a hundred bodies.
If you become a lion, love is a great lion-catcher.
   Become an elephant – love is a mighty rhinoceros!
If you flee to the depths of a well,
   love's rope will bind your neck like a bucket.
Become a hair – love is a great hair-splitter.
   Become a kabob – love is a spit.
Love is the world's sanctuary, the source of all justice,
   even if it waylays the intellects of man and woman.
Silence! For speech's homeland is Damascus, the heart –
   with such a homeland, don't call it a stranger.[27]

★

What would happen, youth, if you became a lover like me –
   every day madness, every night weeping.
His image not out of your eyes for an instant –
   two hundred lights in your eyes from that face.
You would cut yourself off from your friends,
   you would wash your hands of the world:
"I have detached myself from myself,
   I have become totally Yours.
"When I mix with these people, I am water with oil,
   outwardly joined, inwardly separate."
Leaving behind all selfish desires, you would become mad,
   but not any madness a doctor could cure.
If for an instant the physicians tasted this heartache,
   they would escape their chains and tear up their books.
Enough! Leave all this behind, seek a mine of sugar!
   Become effaced in that sugar like milk in pastry.[28]

★

If someone asks you about houris,
    show your face and say, "Like this."
If someone speaks of the moon,
    rise up beyond the roof and say, "Like this."
When someone looks for a fairy princess,
    show your face to him.
When someone talks of musk,
    let loose your tresses and say, "Like this."
If someone says to you,
    "How do clouds part from the moon?"
Undo your robe, button by button,
    and say, "Like this."
If he asks you about the Messiah,
    "How could he bring the dead to life?"
Kiss my lips before him
    and say, "Like this."
When someone says, "Tell me,
    what does it mean to be killed by love?"
Show my soul to him
    and say, "Like this."
If someone out of concern
    asks you about my state,
Show him your eyebrow
    bent over double and say, "Like this."
The spirit breaks away from the body,
    then again it enters within.
Come, show the deniers,
    enter the house and say "Like this."
In whatever direction you hear
    a lover complaining,
That is my story, all of it,
    by God, like this.
I am the house of every angel,
    my breast has turned blue like the sky –

Lift up your eyes and look with joy
   at heaven, like this.
I told the secret of union with the Friend
   to the east wind alone.
Then, through the purity of its own mystery,
   the east wind whispered, "Like this."
Those are blind who say,
   "How can the servant reach God?"
Place the candle of purity in each one's hand
   and say, "Like this."
I said, "How can the fragrance of Joseph
   go from town to town?"
The fragrance of God wafted down
   from His Essence and said, "Like this."
I said, "How can the fragrance of Joseph
   give sight back to the blind?"
Your breeze came and gave light
   to my eyes – "Like this."
Perhaps Shams ad-Din in Tabriz
   will show his generosity,
and in his kindness display
   his good faith, like this.[29]

7

The never-ending dance

When you enter the dance,
   you leave both worlds behind.
The world of the dance
   lies beyond heaven and earth.[1]

During my first year teaching at Stony Brook, a colleague introduced me to a student as the instructor of the new course on Sufism. "Oh, Sufism," she said, "that's dancing, isn't it?" At first I chuckled at her ignorance, but on reconsidering, I thought that she had it just about right.

Westerners first made the connection between Sufism and dancing when travelers brought back tales of the "whirling dervishes" from the Middle East. More recently, many of those who have set themselves up as Sufi teachers have found eager participants in Sufi dancing. By and large, however, dance has played a minor role in Sufism, even in the Mawlawiyya order, where the whirling dance has had a certain importance. Nonetheless, the topic comes up frequently in the texts, and investigating what the Sufi teachers have to say about it can help us in the search for Sufism's reality.

The typical approach of Sufi teaching is to take things back to God. Given that the first principle of faith and understanding is "No god but God," seeing things as they are demands correlating them with their Origin. In order to grasp the reality of dance – that is, its divine archetype – we need to look back to the divine principles that give rise to joyous intoxication and rhythmic movement. In doing so, we can review basic Sufi teachings on the divine names, the image of God, and the path to human perfection.

The divine names

> Neighbor, companion, fellow voyager – all are He.
> In beggar's rags, in king's satin – all are He.
> In the banquet of dispersion and the closet of gathering,
> all are He, by God – by God, all are He![2]

In this quatrain, Jami employs an ecstatic refrain that has been heard in Persian for centuries, at least from the time of Abdullah Ansari (d. 1089). At first sight, "All are He" suggests a kind of simple-minded pantheism, a belief that the sum total of the creatures is identical with God, and many unsympathetic observers have interpreted it in just this sense. But Sufis like Jami were far too sophisticated to consider such exclamations anything more than rhetorical devices aimed at awakening forgetful and negligent human souls to a side of reality that is too often ignored. They never forgot that, if in one sense "All are He," it is even more true in our present situation that "None are He."

If we look at the east of existence, everything displays the divine light. But most people look at the west and see nothing but multiplicity and dispersion. In order to refer this multiplicity back to the One, Muslim thinkers typically have recourse to the divine names. Perhaps the simplest way to understand these is in terms of the sun and its rays. The sun corresponds to God in Himself (called the "Essence" in Islamic theology). The rays of light that emerge from the sun correspond to God's names (also called His "attributes"). The colors and shapes that appear in the world because of the shining of the light are the "signs" of God, or the "creatures," or the eastern faces of things, or, in theological language, God's "acts." Just as a ray of light that enters the room is the sun's act, so also any creature – a tree, a bird, a river, a mountain – is God's act.

If we understand the divine names as jewels, we can read the Hadith of the Hidden Treasure as referring to God's creation of the universe by making manifest His own attributes and qualities. If God had not brought the world into existence, the names would have remained concealed in the treasure chest. Nothing would exist but pure, blinding light, with no one to look and nothing to be seen. According to Ibn Arabi, the divine names are the creative possibilities latent in God, and they are called "storehouses" in the Koranic verse, "There is no thing whose storehouses are not with Us, but We send it down only in a known measure" (15:21).

Rumi compares the universe to a stream of flowing water, "within which shine the attributes of the Majestic."[3] He says,

> The world is foam, God's attributes the ocean –
> the foam veils you from the Ocean's purity![4]

According to Ibn Arabi, "The whole cosmos is the locus of manifestation for the divine names."[5] "In reality," he says, "there is nothing in existence but His names."[6] The line of reasoning here is clear. He is saying that all things come from God, all things manifest God, all things signify God, all things display God, all things are not other than God, "All are He." Or, as he puts it, "There is nothing in existence but God. As for us, though we exist, our existence is through Him. Those who exist through something other than themselves are in fact nonexistent."[7]

To say that the creatures borrow all their existence and attributes from God and that, in themselves, they are "nonexistent," is like saying that the colors and shapes that we perceive everywhere we look show us nothing but the existence and attributes of light. If we look at objects, we seem to see independent and self-subsisting things. Yet we know that we are perceiving only light, which has been given specific colors by the nonexistence of certain other colors. Hence, a single light appears to us in a great variety of hues. In a similar way, the only thing that we perceive in creation is the one reality of God. Nonetheless, the traces and properties of God's names and attributes appear to us in an infinite variety of shapes and forms, and these are called "creatures." As Jami puts it,

> The entities are many-colored windows,
> upon which fall the rays of Being's sun.
> Whether windows be red, blue, or yellow,
> the sun will show itself in that very hue.[8]

God created human beings in His own image or, to follow the Arabic a bit more closely, "upon His form." Sufis often interpreted this to mean that human beings are theaters in which all the names of God display their traces as a unified whole, just as the universe manifests the properties of the names in an infinitely dispersed array. The difference between human beings and other creatures is that each of us is made upon the form of God Himself, thus possessing at least the potential to display the traces and properties of all of God's names as a coherent and integrated whole. Other creatures manifest some of God's names, but not all of them. Only human beings manifest all the jewels of the Hidden Treasure, so only they can know the Treasure in its totality.

Primordial audition

> What is audition? A message from those hidden in the heart.
> The heart, a stranger, finds ease from their missive.
> This breeze makes blossoms bloom on intellect's branch,
> this strumming opens up the pores of all being.[9]

The Koran refers to prophetic revelation in general and to its own verses in particular as "signs," since these give news of God and remind people of their true selves, created in the divine image. It also refers to the creatures and events of the universe as signs, since each of them displays the traces of God's names and attributes. So also, everything within ourselves is a sign of God. "We shall show them Our signs upon the horizons and in their selves" (41:53).

The proper human response to signs is to read them and understand what they say. Many Sufis spoke of three books in which God has written out the full range of His signs – the Koran itself, the cosmos, and the human soul. But the word "Koran" means literally "recitation." Long before it was written down, the Koran was a heard and recited book. The Prophet heard it from Gabriel, and then he recited it to his Companions. So, the signs of God are not only seen, they are also heard. "Surely in that are signs for a people who hear" (10:67).

Hearing the Koran when it is recited is not difficult. But how do we "hear" the signs of the other two books, the universe and the self? How do we avoid being among those concerning whom the Koran says, "They have hearts, but they do not understand with them, and they have ears, but they do not hear with them" (22:46)? In order to hear the signs in the world and the self, is it enough to recognize the divine beauty in the songs of the birds and the beating of the heart? Or do hearing and listening involve something more?

In the Koran God says, "Our only speech to a thing, when We desire, is to say to it 'Be!', so it comes to be" (16:40). In other words, each thing in the universe comes into existence as a result of God's spoken word. In our own case, speech is possible only through breath. On God's part, speech occurs only through the divine Breath known as "the Spirit," the same spirit that was blown into Adam's clay. "Then He proportioned him, and He blew into him of His spirit" (32:9). Ibn Arabi often calls

this Spirit "the Breath of the All-merciful." Within it God articulates His words and immerses all things in the divine mercy,
about which the Koran says, "My mercy embraces everything"
(7:156). The All-merciful Breath is omnipresent existence, a
"mercy for every existent thing,"[10] and a manifestation of God's
love for the Hidden Treasure: "Because of this love to be
known, God breathed, and the Breath became manifest."[11]

> The Breath of the All-merciful bestows existence on the forms
> of the possible things, just as the human breath bestows
> existence on letters. So, the cosmos is God's words in respect of
> this Breath . . . And He has reported that His words will not be
> spent, so His creatures will never cease coming into existence,
> and He will never cease being a Creator.[12]

But how does God say "Be" to something that does not yet
exist? The brief answer runs something like this: before things
come into existence, they possess a certain mode of being in the
storehouses of the unseen world – "There is no *thing* whose
storehouses are not with Us" (15:21). When God says "Be!" to
a thing in one of these storehouses, it hears His command and
obeys. It comes to exist in the world, fulfills the function for
which it was created, and then returns again to the unseen realm.
"Unto God all affairs are returned" (2:210).

In order to come to exist, things need to "hear" *(sama')* God's
command to them. This word *sama'* is also employed to mean
"listening to music" and, by extension, "music." By the end of
the ninth century, listening to music or "audition," as the word
is often translated, had become a practice performed by some of
the Sufis, and typically it was accompanied by dancing. Most
jurists and many Sufis considered the practice a transgression of
the Sharia. Those Sufis who did perform it offered various
Shariite arguments to show that it was legitimate. But, their basic
reason was that they considered it a way to stir up the remembrance of God in the heart. There is something in music, they

said, that can transport people into the invisible world, to their very origin in "nonexistence," to that realm where God is still speaking His eternal word to them.

Ibn Arabi did not encourage audition among his own followers, but he did explain the theory that lies behind the practice. True *sama'*, he tells us, is simply remembrance of the primordial "Be" (*kun*) that brought about the world's "being" (*kawn*) in the first place. The dance that accompanies this remembrance reflects the transferal of things from the storehouses of the unseen realm into the world. "What the Folk of Sama' perceive in the singer's words is God's word *Be* to a thing before it comes to be."[13] The "Folk of Sama'" are those Sufis who employ music to transport themselves into ecstatic states.

> The existence of being's realm is rooted in the divine attribute of speech, for beings know nothing of God but His speech. It is this that they hear, so they enjoy the audition, and they cannot do anything but come to be. Audition naturally disposes the listeners to movement, agitation, and transferal, for when they hear the word *Be*, they are transferred and moved from the state of nonexistence into the state of existence, and thus they come to be. From here derives the root of the movement of the Folk of Sama', who are the folk of ecstasy.[14]

In trying to grasp audition's role in the creation of the universe, we should never forget the role of God's love, which led God to say "Be" in the first place. As the source of the cosmos and its motivating energy, love suffuses all of existence. As Rumi puts it,

> The creatures are set in motion by love,
>   love by God in all eternity –
> The wind dances because of the spheres,
>   the trees because of the wind.[15]

What then did we experience when we heard the word "Be" in our state of nonexistence? We heard a marvelous song, we delighted in its melody, and we danced into the created world. Ever since, each of us has been dancing and reveling in that music, for it fills the universe to overflowing. However, it has such a steady beat that most of us never notice it. Whether or not we do, we never stop dancing. Jami catches the flavor of this omnipresent song in this ghazal:

> Do you know what it is – the sound of lute and rebec?
>> "You are my sufficiency, You are my all, O loving God!"
> The dry and dismal have no taste of *sama'* –
>> otherwise, that song has seized the world.
> Oh that Minstrel! One tune
>> and every atom of being began to dance.
> The ascetic stands on the shore of imagination and fantasy,
>> the gnostic's soul is drowned in the sea of Being.
> The holy threshold of Love has no form,
>> but in every form It shows Itself alone.
> It displayed Itself in the clothing of Layla's beauty,
>> It stole patience and ease from Majnun's heart.
> It tied the veil of Adhra to Its own face,
>> It opened the door of heartache on Wamiq's cheek.
> In reality. It played love with Itself –
>> Wamiq and Majnun are nothing but names.
> Jami saw the reflection of the Cupbearer,
>> then fell to prostration, a pitcher before the cup.[16]

Fakhr ad-Din Iraqi (d. 1289), a student of Ibn Arabi's disciple Qunawi and author of the Persian prose classic *Lama'at* ("Flashes"), offers a slightly more prosaic explanation of how God's command drove all creatures to ecstatic dance:

> The lover was at ease in the being of nonbeing. He was resting in the retreat-house of witnessing, not having seen the Beloved's face. All at once the melody of *Be* stirred him up from the sleep of nonexistence. The audition of that melody

made manifest an ecstasy, and from that ecstasy [*wajd*] he found existence [*wujud*]. The taste of that melody fell to his head – "Love threw turmoil into our soul." After all, "Sometimes the ear falls in love before the eye." Love overmastered the stillness of his outward and inward self with the song of "The lover pays a visit to the one he loves." Then the spirit fell into dance and movement.[17]

Sufis often identify the primordial music heard by the soul with God's words to the children of Adam at the "Covenant of Alast." According to the Koran, when God created Adam as His own vicegerent, He made a covenant with him and his children. "Am I not [*alast*] your Lord?", He asked. They replied, "Yea! We testify" (7:172). Junayd was asked,

> "How is it that a man can be at peace, yet, when he hears the Audition, he becomes agitated?"
>
> He replied, "God addressed Adam's progeny at the Covenant with the words, 'Am I not your Lord?' All their spirits were immersed in the enjoyment of those words. When they hear the Audition in this world, they enter into movement and agitation."[18]

If Junayd, the pillar of sober Sufism, could acknowledge the intoxicating power of *sama'*, then it is not surprising to see that Rumi, the leader of Sufism's drunken rowdies, makes the music of Alast a frequent theme of his poetry. In this ghazal, he is addressing those who have formally entered the Sufi path, but are afraid to give themselves up to the Beloved.

> You're still caught up with arranging your shoes and turban –
> how can you lift the cup of the heavy drinker?
> By my soul, come for a moment to the tavern!
> You too are Adam's child, you're human, you have a soul.
> Come, pawn your cloak with the wine-merchant of Alast,
> for he's been selling wine from Alast, before water and clay.

You call yourself a fakir, a gnostic, a dervish – then stay sober?
  These names are metaphors, you're imagining things.
Are not Audition and *He gives to drink* [76:21] the dervish's
  work?
  Are not loss and profit, little and much, the merchant's work?
Come on, tell me, what is Alast? Everlasting joy.
  Don't delay with all this ceremony, you're all set to go.
If your head has no pain, why do you bind it up?
  If your body has no suffering, why pretend to be sick?[19]

Human perfection

The bats of darkness
  dance in their love for shadows,
the birds of the sun
  dance from dawn to *the day's brightness* [93:1].[20]

When the Minstrel played His tune, the creatures danced into existence, displaying the jewels of the Hidden Treasure and showing that "All are He." But the dance is not yet complete. God said that He loved "to be known" by His creatures. There are degrees of knowledge here, and none of us should ever think that we know enough.

No doubt all things possess a certain knowledge of God by the fact that they exist. The Koran says in several verses that "Everything in the heavens and the earth glorifies God," and "glorification" is not an unconscious act. As Ibn Arabi writes,

God created no being unless living and rationally speaking, whether it be an inanimate thing, a plant, or an animal, in the higher or the lower world. The proof text of this is His words, *There is nothing that does not glorify Him in praise, but you do not understand their glorification* [17:44].[21]

Rumi tells us that those who actualize self-knowledge and join with the ranks of the gnostics hear the speech of all things.

> The speech of water, the speech of earth, the speech of clay –
> all are perceived by the Folk of Heart.[22]

Each creature was created with its own sort of knowledge and speech, and this allows it to utter the praise of God. But human beings, made upon God's form, were created to know God in respect of all His names and attributes, and unlike the knowledge possessed by other creatures, this knowledge does not arise as a matter of course. If people are to remember what they know innately, they need to engage their free wills to search for it. This is precisely the significance of the Covenant of Alast, when Adam's children accepted to carry God's Trust. Ibn Arabi writes,

> "God created Adam upon His form," so He ascribed to him all
> of His own most beautiful names. Through the strength of
> these names he was able to carry the Trust offered to him. The
> reality of his divine form did not allow him to reject the Trust,
> as did the heavens, the earth and the mountains, all of which
> refused to carry it.[23]

Only when people have realized the divine form can they understand the true significance of "All are He." In the meantime, they remain ignorant of their own true nature, and they continue to live as if "None are He." In order to fulfill their human potential, they need to enter the path to God. The later Sufis call those who traverse this path and achieve their true human status "perfect human beings" *(insan kamil)*. In reaching perfection they are following in the footsteps of their father Adam, whom God created in His own form, making him the locus of manifestation for His own all-comprehensive name. This is the name God (Allah), which embraces and includes all the ninety-nine most beautiful names. As Ibn Arabi says, "Adam emerged in the form of the name *God,* because this name contains all the divine names. Thus the human being, though small in body, contains all the meanings."[24] Since God has let us know that Adam alone was created in His form, "It is as if He is saying, 'All My names become manifest only in the human configuration.'"[25]

All Adam's children were created upon the form of God, so all have the potential to attain perfection. The Sufis often quote the Prophet as saying, "Assume the character traits of God!" In other words, adopt as your own the properties and characteristics of God's names and attributes. Once people achieve the perfection of the divine form, they become microcosms or "small worlds," gathering in their own souls all the realities that are dispersed throughout the cosmos. As Ghazali puts it,

> God showed beneficence to Adam. He gave him an abridged form that brings together every sort of thing found in the cosmos. It is as if Adam is everything in the cosmos, or an abridged transcription of the world.[26]

Ibn Arabi often explains human perfection as the realization of the divine form and the actualization of the correspondence between the human being and the universe. Here are two examples:

> Within human beings is the potential of every existent thing in the cosmos, so they possess all the levels. This is why they alone were singled out for the Form. They bring together the divine realities, which are the names, and the realities of the cosmos, since they are the last existent thing . . . In human beings becomes manifest that which does not become manifest in the separate parts of the cosmos, nor in the separate names among the divine realities, for each of the names does not bestow what the others bestow in respect of distinctiveness. Hence, human beings are the most perfect existent things.[27]

★

God did not create human beings *for sport* [23:115]. On the contrary. He created them alone to be upon His form. Hence everyone in the cosmos is ignorant of the whole and knows the part, except only the perfect human being. For God *taught him the names, all of them* [2:31] and He gave him the all-comprehensive words, so his form became perfect. The perfect human being brings together the form of the Real and the form of the cosmos. He is an isthmus between the Real and the cosmos, a raised-up mirror. The Real sees His form in the mirror of the human being, and creation also see its form in him. Those who gain this level have gained a level of perfection more perfect than which nothing is found in possibility.[28]

Perfect human beings realize the human potential to be one of the three divine books. It is not enough for those who want to follow in their footsteps to hear God's signs in the two outside books – the Koran and the universe. The human self is the greatest of all books, for it alone allows God to achieve His goal in creating the world. Both the universe and the Koran are means to achieve the goal, but neither has the potential to become a self-aware book. Both manifest the Hidden Treasure, but neither can know it with full awareness. Qunawi employs the imagery of the book in encouraging a young disciple to pursue the path of self-knowledge:

The perfect human being is a book that comprehends all the divine and cosmic books. We said concerning the Real that His knowledge of His Essence entails His knowledge of all things, and that He knows all things by knowing His Essence. In the same way, we say concerning the perfect human being that his knowledge of his essence entails his knowledge of all things and that he knows all things by knowing his essence. This is because he is all things, in both undifferentiation and differentiation.

So, "He who knows himself knows his Lord" and he also knows all things. So, my son, if you reflect upon yourself, that is enough for you, since there is nothing outside of you. The leader of the gnostics, Ali ibn Abi Talib, said,

> Your cure is within you, but you do not know,
>> your illness is from you, but you do not see.
> You are the "Clarifying Book"
>> through whose letters becomes manifest the hidden.
> You suppose that you're a small body
>> but the greatest world unfolds within you.
> You would not need what is outside yourself
>> if you would reflect upon self, but you do not reflect.

In the same way, [Ibn Arabi,] the seal of the specific, Muhammadan sanctity said,

> I am the Koran and the *seven oft-repeated* [15:87],
>> and the spirit of the spirit – there is no spirit I am not.

Have you not heard the words of God? *Read your book! Your self suffices you this day as a reckoner against you!* [17:14]. Whoso reads this book has come to know what has been, what is, and what will be. If you cannot read all of your book, read of it what you can. Have you not seen how He says, *And in your selves: What, do you not look?* [51:21]. And have you not seen how He says, *We shall show them Our signs in the horizons and in their selves, till it is clear to them that it is the truth. Suffices it not as to your Lord, that He is witness over everything?* [41:53] . . .

It has been recounted that when Ali's army gained the upper hand over A'isha's army (peace be upon them both!) in the battle that took place after the slaying of Uthman, A'isha's party held the Divine Book aloft with a spear so that Ali's followers would not slay and rout them. When they saw this happen, they left the battle. Then Ali said, "O people! I am the *speaking*

Book of God, but that is the *silent* Book of God! Attack them and leave them not!"

In the same way God says. *Say: "God suffices as a witness between me and you, and whosoever possesses knowledge of the Book"* [13:43]. So this, my son, is the Book and the knowledge of the Book. And you are the Book, as we said. Your knowledge of yourself is your knowledge of the Book. *And there is not a thing, neither wet*, which is the visible world, *nor dry*, which is the spiritual world and everything beyond, *but in a Clarifying Book* [6:59], and that is you.[29]

The ascent of the soul

For a time you were the elements,
for a time an animal.
Now you have been a spirit,
so become the Beloved! Become the Beloved![30]

Created upon God's form, human beings have the potential to participate with total awareness in the infinite unfolding of the traces and properties of God's names. The Koran often expresses astonishment at those who look upon the signs in the cosmos and themselves and do not recognize that everything is built on transformation and change, all with a view toward the full realization of what things truly are. Death and resurrection are but two further stages of the growth that begins in the womb. "O people, if you are in doubt as to the Resurrection – surely We created you of dust, then of a sperm-drop, then of a blood-clot . . . And We establish in the wombs what We will, till a stated term. Then We deliver you as infants, then that you may come of age" (22:5).

The Sufis see the stages of physical life as the outward signs of the soul's blossoming and unfolding. Rumi is well-known for his description of the soul's growth from a stage that is practically inanimate to one that surpasses the angels. The fact that the soul ascends stage by stage explains why, even though "All are He," no one can truly be aware of this without achieving perfection. As long as people have not passed through the levels of moral and spiritual growth, they will remain ignorant of their own true nature.

The journey toward perfection begins in "nonexistence" with God. Once people hear the command "Be" and acknowledge God at the Covenant of Alast, they descend level by level until they enter into the womb, which is the point of creation furthest from the Origin. Then they begin their ascent to God, for all things return to Him, just as all things have come from Him. The two journeys – from God to the world and from the world to God – are often called the two "arcs" of the Circle of Existence.

In one sense the return to God is compulsory, since it represents the natural unfolding of the creative process, and no one has any choice in the matter. "To Him has submitted whoso is in the heavens and in the earth, willingly or unwillingly, and to Him they shall be returned" (3:83). But there is also a voluntary return that is the prerogative of human beings, since they alone, made upon God's form, have been given a sufficient share of the divine freedom to shape their own destinies. Only humans are addressed by the prophets, who provide instructions on how to return to God willingly, before they are taken to Him through death. Only humans have accepted to carry the Trust.

Human beings have two perfections. The first perfection can be called "natural," and it leads to physical death and then to the resurrection and the meeting with God. "O Man! You are laboring unto your Lord laboriously, and you shall encounter Him" (84:6). The second perfection can only be achieved through the voluntary cultivation of the soul. From the first standpoint, people are compelled to grow and die, but from the second they are free to choose what sort of existence they will experience in the next stages of becoming.

The natural growth of the soul begins in the womb, when God blows His own spirit into the body. This spirit, which descends by way of the realm of Alast, is a pure and living light, and the body is dark and dead clay. The conjunction of spirit and body gives rise to the soul proper, which embraces both worlds, the spiritual and the corporeal. The soul is the intermediary through which the pure and transcendent spirit is put into contact with the corruptible body. It is the sum total of the life and consciousness that is born at the meeting of light and clay. It is the self that is immersed in the world, yet inwardly open to the Infinite.

The spirit is a ray of divine awareness described by all God's attributes. It can only manifest its properties by means of a body, just as the Hidden Treasure can only be known through a cosmos. When a person is born, the perfections latent in the divine names begin to display themselves in the soul, which links spirit and body. Here again light offers a useful analogy. Spirit is unmixed, intelligible light, and body is sheer darkness. When light and darkness mix, the myriad colors appear to the eyes, displaying the inherent properties of light. In the soul, the spirit's life, knowledge, desire, and power assume specific, individual characteristics. Each person's soul becomes distinct from everyone else's, though all are created from the single divine spirit, the All-merciful Breath.

During the soul's unfolding, the traces of the divine names manifest themselves gradually. Many Sufis (as well as many of the Muslim philosophers) compare the fetus in its early stages to an inanimate object or mineral. Little by little the properties of life and sensation appear within it until it reaches the stage of a plant. By the time the child is born, it has acquired all the attributes of an animal, though imperfectly. It is not until around the time of puberty, when the highest human faculties – intelligence and speech – begin to display their possibilities, that a person deserves to be called a "human being," though provisionally. In fact we all remain less than human until we achieve the full realization of the divine names within ourselves.

The natural unfolding of the soul can never take people to perfection, because it does not ask for the engagement of free will and the carrying of the Trust. Certainly, we all return to God, but how will this return take place? Will we return to God's mercy or His wrath, to felicity or chastisement, to paradise or hell? As Ibn Arabi likes to point out, people will return to the specific divine names whose traces they have actualized during their sojourn in the world, and they should not forget the differing properties and characteristics of the names.

> The properties of the divine names, in respect of being names, are diverse. What do Avenger, Terrible in Punishment, and Overpowering have in common with Compassionate, Forgiving, and Gentle? For Avenger demands the occurrence of vengeance in its object, and Compassionate demands the removal of vengeance from the same object.[31]

The Sharia makes the practice of the religion incumbent upon children when they reach puberty, that is, when intelligence (the divine attribute of "knowledge") has sufficiently developed to discern between right and wrong. The prescriptions of the Sharia allow for the actualization of certain potentialities of the divine form that could not appear without a clear choice between right and wrong and the free acceptance of the Trust. The goal is for each of the divine names to be realized in the soul in perfect harmony with all the others.

If Sufism differs from non-Sufi Islam in its vision of the soul's development, this is because the Sufi teachers have a better understanding of the goal and the seriousness of the quest. There are always people who feel drawn to God in the present life, who do not have the patience to remain separate from their beloved until death. They follow the command of the Prophet, "Die before you die!" By dying to their own individual limitations, they are born into the unlimited expanse of the divine beauty. They have no fear of death, since they have died many times, and each time they have been reborn as something better. Rumi explains this in some of his most famous verses:

> I died as a mineral and became a plant,
>> I died as a plant and became an animal.
> I died as an animal and became a man.
> Why should I fear?
>> When did I ever become less through dying?
> Next time I will die to human nature,
>> spreading *my* wings and lifting up my head with the angels.
> Then I will jump the stream of angelic nature,
>> for *Everything is perishing but His Face* [28:88].
> Once I am sacrificed as an angel,
>> I will become what does not enter the imagination.
> I will become nothing, for nonexistence plays the tune,
>> *Unto Him we shall return* [2:156].[32]

This entrance into "nonexistence" is a return to the original human situation, when we dwelt at peace with God before creation. This is the state that is sometimes called the "annihilation" of the ego's limitations and the "subsistence" of the true self. Annihilation is to realize the "No god" of the Shahadah by negating everything other than God. Subsistence is to realize "but God" by affirming the divine attributes whose traces shine in the soul. Before annihilation, the soul's eyes are fixed on the western side of existence and cannot see the sun. Through subsistence, the sun rises from the western horizon in which it had set, and nothing remains but the shining light of God. As Rumi explains,

> *Everything is perishing but His Face* –
>> since you are not in His Face, do not seek to be.
> "When someone is annihilated in Our Face,
>> *Everything is perishing* no longer applies to him.

"For he is in *but God*, he has passed beyond *no god*.
Whoever is in *but* has not been annihilated."[33]

Through love for God and surrender to Him by following the Prophet's Sunnah, the travelers leave the west of existence and enter the east of the risen sun, where nothing appears but the rays of God's names and attributes. It is here that they actualize the Prophet's command to assume God's character traits as their own. Qunawi describes this ascent to God as the shucking off of creaturely limitations, stage by stage:

> The gnostic travels toward the upper world, and from the time he departs from the earth he never passes by any element, presence, or celestial sphere without discarding within it the part of himself that corresponds to it – the part that he acquired when he first came [into the world]. Thus he obeys God's words, *God commands you to deliver trusts back to their owners* [4:58].[34]

Qunawi explains that when the travelers reach the name God, upon the form of which they were created, they become established in the precedent names of mercy and gentleness. These designate what he calls the "center point of the circle" or the "point of equilibrium." Failing to stand at the center means falling to the periphery of existence, which is the domain of wrath and severity.

> Those who leave the equilibrium of this middle, center point – which is the point of perfection in the presence of the all-comprehensive unity – will be judged in respect of their distance from or nearness to the center. Some will be near and some nearer, some far and some farther. Between the complete disequilibrium specific to satanity and this divine, name-derived, perfect equilibrium become designated all the levels of the folk of felicity and the folk of wretchedness.[35]

The music of the spheres

> In our lines of battle, we hold up no shield,
>> in our Audition, we know nothing of flute and drum.
> Annihilated in His love, we're dirt beneath His feet,
>> love through and through, love all in all, we are nothing else.[36]

In returning to God voluntarily, the Sufis seek to realize the full range and total equilibrium of the divine names – or to assume as their own the traits of the name God, which comprehends all the names. They reach the goal by *dhikr*. Only by remembering God, by turning their minds and their whole existence toward Him in whose form they were created, can they hope to become god-like in a true sense. As Rumi says, "God will give you what you seek. Where your aspiration lies, that you will become, for 'The bird flies with its wings, but the believer flies with his aspiration.'"[37] Constant remembrance of God fans the fire of love in the heart.

> In the outside world, wind sets the trees in motion –
>> On the inside, remembrance rustles the leaves of the heart.[38]

The goal of the Audition is to strengthen the remembrance of God and to fan the flames that burn away everything but the Beloved. For the Folk of Sama', music is the secret language of God's luminous, audible signs. Hearing it, the soul recalls its original abode in the days of Alast, when nearness to God was its natural home. As Rumi puts it,

> Philosophers say that we've taken
>> these melodies from the revolution of the spheres.
> The songs people sing with lute and throat
>> are the sounds of the spheres in their turning . . .
> We were all parts of Adam,
>> we heard those melodies in paradise.
> Water and clay have covered us with doubt,
>> but we still remember something of those tunes . . .

So Audition is the food of lovers –
    within it they find the image of union.[39]

Rumi's contemporary Najm ad-Din Razi explains the attraction of music in terms of the Covenant of Alast:

> When a Real-seeing eye and a Real-hearing ear appear in the soul and when it finds once again the taste of inspirations, then, wherever there is a correspondence, it finds the taste of the inspirations from the Unseen, and it will move toward the Real. Thus God says, *Those who hear the word and follow the most beautiful of it* [39:18]. Hence, whenever the soul hears the singer sing words clothed in sweet garments and measured rhythms, it tastes the address of Alast. This sweet sound causes a movement of yearning toward the Real . . . Once the soul finds the taste of this address, the bird of the spirit cannot rest, and it falls into agitation. It tries to smash the cage of the bodily frame and to return to its own world . . . As a result, the cage of the frame falls into agitation. "Dancing" and [spiritual] "states" consist of this agitation.[40]

Ruzbihan Baqli (d. 1209), one of the more intoxicated among the Sufi prose writers, describes the state of the spiritual traveler who contemplates the unseen world and listens to its primordial music:

> When the gnostic turns his hearing toward the Unseen of the unseen, the light of sudden witnessing falls into the core of his secret heart and his spirit encounters the beauty of the Real in the clothing of contentment and joyful expansion. His spirit delights in God and it almost flies from the human makeup. It remains imprisoned and bewildered in the jail of the original disposition. As much as the light of the Real becomes unveiled to it, it inclines toward ascending to the Realm of Sovereignty. With its form it drags its tail in this world. Because of delight in God, it is described as dancing, moving, turning, and so on.

The speed in which the brilliance of the attributes fall give it the attribute of rejoicing. All this is because it has found the object of its desire – the vision of the attributes and the specific hearing of the [divine] address . . . The gnostic says, "Dancing is the fluctuation of the spirit in the shrine of eternity without beginning, since it sees the existence of the Real in the clothing of beauty."[41]

Dancing, then, expresses the travelers' joy at release from individual selfhood. Razi explains that the soul's agitation throws the body into turmoil.

Dancing is not to keep jumping up,
    floating in air without pain like dust.
Dancing is to jump out from the two worlds –
    to shatter your heart, to leap from your soul![42]

Rumi tells us that the dance of Sufis takes place in their own hearts and spirits. It is the joyful resurrection of the subsistent soul after the annihilation of its own imperfections.

People dance and frolic in the square –
    Men dance in their own blood.
Freed from their own hands, they clap their hands.
    Having leapt from their own imperfections, they dance.
Within them their minstrels beat their tambourines –
    their uproar makes the ocean clap its waves.[43]

Dancing, then, has no necessary connection with the body, since it is experienced by the soul that has been delivered from limitations. True music cannot be heard by imperfect ears, and the dance of the Men – the true Sufis, whether they be men or women – cannot be observed with the eyes. The distinction between ordinary people and those who have set out on the path to God remains basic to the texts. One should never suppose that Sufis prescribe music and dance for everyone, quite the contrary. Even Sufis who approved of it acknowledged its ambiguous status. Dhu'n-Nun al-Misri (d. 861) made the point in the typical aphoristic style of the early texts, and his words have echoed down through the centuries:

> Audition is an influx from God with which He stirs up the hearts and encourages them to search for Him. Whoever hears it through the Real finds the road to the Real, and whoever hears it through the self falls into heresy.[44]

In a chapter on *sama'* in one of his many books, Ruzbihan explains that not everyone is qualified to listen to music:

> All existing and living things incline toward Audition, for each has a spirit appropriate to itself through which it is alive, and this spirit lives through Audition. Audition refreshes all thoughts from the heaviness of mortal humanity. It excites the natures in human beings and brings the Lordly mysteries into movement. For some it is a seduction, because they are incomplete, and for some it is a pointer, because they are complete. Those who are alive through nature and dead in the heart should not listen to the Audition, for it will bring destruction down upon them.[45]

If the status of music is ambiguous, that of dancing is even more so. The true dance takes place in another world, even if, on occasion, it displays its traces in the visible realm. This helps explain the derision in Ruzbihan's words:

> A group of the delirious dance, recite poetry, perform the Audition, clap their hands, and tear their clothing, imagining that, having achieved this, they have found the states of God's friends. What nonsense! How can the stations [of perfection] be found through such fabrications?[46]

Jami, one of the greatest exponents of the idea of the Unity of Being *(wahdat al-wujud)* and the author of a good deal of ecstatic poetry, expresses similar disgust at the excesses of certain self-proclaimed Sufis:

> The imperfect dance toward imperfection,
>   but the movement of the perfect is not "dance."
> The spirit of the perfect flaps its wings,
>   freeing itself from the depths of harm.
> A single sound makes both groups
>   leap up for the *sama'*,
> But these spread their mantle over the spheres,
>   and those descend down into the earth.
> These rub their heads against the highest heaven,
>   those take their beds beneath the ground.
> The wretched owl sits next to the falcon,
>   but when the two take to the sky,
> The falcon finds its house in the king's castle,
>   the owl goes back to a corner of the ruins.
> Every person inclines toward his own home,
>   every bird flies to its own nest . . .
> They show no spark of remembrance's light,
>   no trace of Audition's state.
> Their remembrance pains their heads and necks,
>   their dancing weakens their bellies and backs.[47]

Dancing with God

> Come, come, for You are the spirit of the spirit of Audition's
>   spirit!
> Come, for You are a walking cypress in Audition's garden!
> Come, for no one like You has ever been or ever will be!
>   Come, for the eyes of Audition have never seen the likes of
>   You![48]

When the Sufis follow the long path back to their Beloved, they pass through numerous "states" of the soul – hope and fear, joy and sorrow, expansion and contraction, intoxication and sobriety – and they acquire the "stations" that are the soul's virtues, character traits, and perfections. These states and stations have been described in detail in many Sufi works. In the long poem *The Language of the Birds* – one of the most famous, and at the same time entertaining accounts of the spirit's journey in Sufi literature – Attar tells how the birds gathered together and decided to travel to their king, the Phoenix. Guided by the hoopoe and undergoing many adventures on the way, they flew across seven valleys – aspiration, love, knowledge, independence, unity, bewilderment, and annihilation – before finally reaching their goal. Other Sufis have numbered the stages of the journey as ten, forty, one hundred, three hundred, or even one thousand. The best I can do here by way of describing the journey is to offer a glimpse of the effect of its wine on those who have drunk it. First, a ghazal from Attar:

> Tonight I'll set out half drunk,
>> my feet dancing, a cup of dregs in my hand.
> I'll turn my head to the scoundrels' market
>> and in one hour lose everything there is.
> How long will I display myself falsely?
>> How long in fancy will I worship self?
> The curtain of fancy must be torn,
>> the repentance of ascetics must be smashed!
> The time has come for me to clap my hands –
>> how long will I remain bound in foot?
> O Cupbearer, give me the heart-opening wine right now –
>> my heart has left me, sorrow sits in my head!
> Send the cup around so that we, like Men,
>> may bring the wheel of heaven under our feet.
> We will tear off Jupiter's cloak
>> and intoxicate Venus until the resurrection.

Like Attar, we will leave all the directions
    and begin dancing in the directionless because of Alast.[49]

Rumi speaks of the same "directionless" domain as "No-place"
– the true "Utopia" of the soul. "Wine" may be an adequate
symbol to suggest the drunkenness that overcomes the travelers
when they enter the Beloved's embrace, but, as Rumi suggests
here, there is much more to the experience of annihilation and
subsistence than mere intoxication.

I know nothing of that wine – I'm annihilated.
    I've gone too far into No-place to know where I am.
Sometimes I fall to the depths of an ocean,
    then I rise up again like the sun.
Sometimes I make a world pregnant,
    sometimes I give birth to a world of creation.
Like a parrot, my soul nibbles on sugar,
    then I become drunk and nibble the parrot.
I can't be held by any place in the world,
    I know nothing but that placeless Friend.
I'm a drunken rascal, totally mad –
    among all the rascals, I make the most noise.
You say to me, "Why don't you come to yourself?"
    You show me myself, I'll come to it.
The shadow of the Phoenix has caressed me so much
    that you'd say I'm the Phoenix, he's the shadow.
I saw beauty drunk, and it kept on saying,
    "I'm affliction, I'm affliction, I'm affliction."
A hundred souls answered it from every direction –
    "I'm yours, I'm yours, I'm yours!
"You're that light that kept on saying to Moses,
    I'm God, I'm God, I'm God."
I said: "Shams of Tabriz, who are you?"
    He said: "I'm you, I'm you, I'm you."[50]

If this is what the Sufis find when they drink the wine of God, is it any wonder that they can do nothing but dance? Rumi describes the ruckus they raise:

> Again we've come back from the tavern drunk,
>   again we're freed from ups and from downs.
> All the drunkards are happily dancing,
>   clap your hands, pretty girls, clap, clap!
> The fish and the sea have both become drunk –
>   the hook is the tip of Your lovely tresses.
> They've turned the tavern upside down,
>   upset the vats, smashed the jars.
> When the shaykh of the tavern saw the tumult,
>   he went up to the roof and jumped.
> A wine began to bubble
>   and being became nonbeing, nonbeing being.
> The glass broke and the pieces scattered –
>   look at the drunkards who've cut their feet!
> Where are those who can't tell their feet from their heads?
>   They've fallen down drunk in the lane of Alast.
> The wine-worshipers are all busy with revelry –
>   listen to the *tan-tan-i tan-tan*, you body-worshipers![51]

The human soul begins its journey in the lower world as the link between the lifeless body and the luminous spirit. It realizes the fullness of its own nature when it returns to the divine source from which it came. Having begun as an infinite potentiality, it grows by assuming the traits of all the divine names as its own. The travelers on God's path come to know all creation within their own souls, for they travel in a microcosm that embraces all things and all worlds. They keep on ascending in spiritual degrees until, having reached God, they begin the never-ending journey in God and with God.

Ibn Arabi reminds us that the Koran says "He is with you wherever you are" (57:4), not that we are with Him wherever

He is. What distinguishes perfect human beings is precisely that they are always with God. "Perfect human beings . . . travel with their Lord through a divine unveiling and a realized witthness whereby they are with the Real, just as God is *with* us *wherever we are*."[52] Having entered the shoreless oceans of their own selves, they travel with God wherever He goes.

> They accompany the divine names in the journey of the names into being. They accompany the realm of being in its journey from nonexistence to existence. They accompany the prophets in their journeys, so they accompany Adam in his journey from the Garden to the earth . . . So also [they accompany] every prophet and angel, like the journeys of Gabriel to every prophet and messenger . . . and the journey of the [divine] self-disclosure in its forms, until they become aware of the realities of all this – all through a tasting in themselves.[53]

They remain with God and all things in this world and the next, free of the limitations of time and space, enjoying the constant flux of the never-repeated disclosures of knowledge and bliss. When they reach the utmost limits of the path, they enter the oceans of divine knowledge, where all is bewilderment – not the bewilderment of being lost, but the bewilderment of having found all and everything in an endless outpouring.[54] "Guidance," says Ibn Arabi, "is to be led to bewilderment. Then you will know that the whole affair is bewilderment, that bewilderment is agitation and movement, and movement is life. There is no rest, no death, only existence, nothing of nonexistence."[55]

So it continues for all eternity. In reality, it is this bewilderment that allows the Sufis to taste already in this world the never-ending bliss of paradise.

> In paradise, at every instant there is a new creation and a new bliss, so boredom never occurs. After all, when anything happens in a natural domain continually and without change,

people become bored, for this is their essential attribute. If God did not nourish them with renewal at every moment so that they might have bliss in that, boredom would overcome them. So, with every glance that they cast toward their kingdoms, the folk of paradise perceive things and forms that they had never seen before, and thus they increase in bliss. Each time they eat or drink they find new and delicious flavors that they had never tasted before.[56]

Already in this world the perfect Sufis live with God. They journey into the Infinite, listening to the music of God's creative command. At each moment God says "Be" and a new self-disclosure, more glorious and perfect than the preceding, delights the eye. In the words of Iraqi,

> The song will never cease, nor the dance come to an end, for all eternity, because the Beloved is infinite. Here the lover hums,
>
> > The moment I open my eyes,
> >   I see Your face,
> > The instant I lend an ear,
> >   I hear Your voice.
>
> So, the lover continues to dance and to move, even though he may appear to be still. *You will see the mountains that you suppose fixed passing by like clouds* [27:88]. How could he remain still? Each atom of the universe prods him to move – each atom is a word, each word speaks a name, each name has a different tongue, and each tongue has a song. For each song the lover has an ear. Pay attention – the singer and the listener are one. *"Sama' is* a bird that flies from God to God."[57]

8

Images of beatitude

Although the Sufis sing of God's presence most often in their poetry, many of them employed prose for the same ends. Among these, few have succeeded as well as Baha Walad (d. 1230), whose name has been seen, if not remembered, by everyone who has read an account of the life of Rumi, his illustrious son. We are told that Baha Walad was a preacher and scholar in Balkh. Hearing of the approaching Mongol invasion, he set out with his family for Mecca and eventually ended up in Konya as "sultan of the learned." He wrote a book called *Ma'arif* ("Gnostic Sciences"), but few have paid much attention to it. Among Orientalists, A. J. Arberry called it a "precious record" of "mystical experiences . . . described in remarkably fine and eloquent Persian," and he translated the first twenty chapters into English, about five percent of the text.[1] What is especially unusual about *Ma'arif* is the manner in which Baha Walad speaks of the spiritual life in intimate, first-person terms. The only work I know that might be compared to it is the Arabic *Kashif al-asrar* ("The Unveiler of the Mysteries") by his contemporary Ruzbihan Baqli, a relatively short treatise that is now available in English translation.[2] However, Ruzbihan couches his book in a more literary language, and he describes a visionary realm of extraordinary apparitions. The reader is left with a strong sense of God's otherness and inaccessibility, and few would feel called to follow Ruzbihan in his path. He constantly lets readers know that he has been granted truly remarkable privileges. In contrast, Baha Walad invites his readers to share in his vision of the holiness and luminosity of all creation.

Baha Walad's book is certainly not a systematic study of Sufi learning, despite what the title might suggest. It is rather a series of meditations, each beginning with a phrase or verse from the Koran, a hadith, a saying, or a recollection. But more than anything else, it is a record of encounters with God in the little details of everyday life. Perhaps it can best be compared to Rumi's prose work, *Fihi ma fthi* ("In it is what is in it"), which is also a compilation of scattered thoughts about a variety of topics. But *Fihi ma fihi* takes the form of conversations that were collected by Rumi's disciples. *Ma'arif* is a record of thoughts that Baha Walad himself put down on paper.

In his introduction to the critical edition of the text, the incomparable scholar of Rumi Badi'uz-Zaman Furuzanfar describes in some detail the parallels between Baha Walad's prose and Rumi's poetry. A thorough study of these could easily fill a book. There is little doubt that *Ma'arif is* the single most important literary influence on Rumi after the Koran and the Hadith. The hagiographical accounts tell us that Rumi used to read the book constantly before the coming of Shams-i Tabrizi, and it was only after Shams's disappearance that Rumi began to compose poetry. It was as if separation from Shams threw the ocean of imagery, much of it already given form by Baha Walad's *Ma'arif*, into tumult, rhythm, and meter.

The vision of God

The Kalam experts say that people will not be given the vision (*ru'ya*) of God until they reach paradise, but Baha Walad tells us that those who have faith are already seeing Him, whether they recognize Him or not. In one passage, he explains that the formula "Glory be to God," usually taken as the assertion of God's transcendence and the impossibility of seeing Him, means in fact that God is seen everywhere.

I was saying, *Glory be to Thee* [2:32]. This means: You are pure and far from defect – the defect that the creatures imagine, that my parts imagine, and that all the parts of the world imagine. [They imagine that] You are not powerful, You are not knowing, and You do not exercise control over them. They say that these parts do not see You, for they do not see how You give being to these parts, make them low, and make them high. They say that You create the parts of the eyes' light, but these do not see You. You give being to the parts of the intellect, awareness, and perception, but these do not see You.

No, no. *Glory be to Thee* means that You are pure of and far above the defect of words like this that they say – that each part does not see You. How can they know You if they have not seen You? Without seeing, knowing You is impossible. Those who deny the seeing of You have not known You. How can anyone incline to service if the seeing of You is not before him? This is the "withness" of *And He is with you wherever you are* [57:4]. O parts, unless there is seeing, withness is impossible! It seems that unbelief is not to see You, and Islam is to see You.[3]

Baha Walad constantly tells us that every sweet and desirable thing in both worlds rises up from the experience of God's presence, though people are confused by the multiplicity of the names and think that the things are the realities. He questions the well-known proposition that paradise is the prison of the Sufi, who desires only God himself.

I was describing the houris and talking about the gardens and the paradises. A shaykh from among the Folk of Gnosis said, "Those who are busy with these things in this world will be busy with them in that world too. When will they go back to God? When will they see God?"

I answered, "It is proper that the 'houris, palaces, gardens, fountains, and ginger' [mentioned in the Koran] consist of the states of seeing God. Each time you see, you find a different taste. So, look upon the meanings – how God constantly keeps you in the palm of His hand and His breast. Belong to your Lord and be His companion! Be a stranger to other things and other states. Keep your gaze upon your Sovereign. Whatever you want, ask it from Him. Rub yourself against Him. Mix with Him like milk and honey. Then you will find all the houris, palaces, and sweetnesses of paradise in ready coin. You will find God. Your felicity is for this door to be opened to you – for you to know that *He is with you wherever you are*.[4]

For Baha Walad, as for Rumi, the vision of God in all creation takes place in infinite variety and never-ending joy. Both attempt to describe the diversity of forms within which they perceive the divine self-disclosure, and it is here that poetical imagery is born. The vision of God takes place at the level of "thought" (*andisha*) – which as Rumi makes clear, is identical with "imagination" (*khayal*)[5] – *so* the mind of the visionary becomes a fountain of fresh and ever-renewed images overflowing into language. Baha Walad describes how his thoughts take on imaginal form in many passages. One soon reaches the conclusion that everything he says fits into a radiant tapestry woven of the ceaseless images of God's self-showing.

Thought is like a wellspring that God causes to bubble up. If sweet water bubbles up, I see that green herbs, bounties, and flowers spring up in the body's sanctuary, and water goes in every direction in the body's earth. But if salty water bubbles up, the body's earth becomes salty and without profit. I keep on looking at God to see which sort of water He will give to the body's earth.[6]

*

I was thinking that these parts of mine have found several thousand neighbors. These words of my thoughts, like green herbs and saffron – from which breast have they sprung up? Or like ants – on whose colored cheeks have they scrambled out, tripping over one another in my breast? Then I saw that God is working alone behind this curtain of the Unseen. He keeps everyone according to His desire. He gives no one a path to Him, whether angel, prophet, saint, wrongdoer, or wronged. No one becomes cognizant of how He works. From there He sends out commands to everyone. He judges and determines. He does not let anyone work according to his own desire. He has made impossibility and howness into Alexander's wall, so that no one may pass beyond it. He has tied a knot at the end of everyone's conceptualizing and imagining so that no one may come out of it. Everyone who takes a step outside that boundary is plundered such that he ceases to be. A cold strikes against him and freezes him, or a hot wind blows over him and burns him up Then I saw that the world is like a house and a pavilion that God has brought out. He has sent out my meanings on its inside, like aware individuals, as if the servants of a king are sitting and standing in the pavilions and porches. My substances are like the walls of the houses, within which the meanings walk. The world is sweet for those who find it like Eden. After all, how should I not be happy? God does all my acts. He by Himself makes and gives being to my earth, my air, and all my atoms. I see that all my parts are happily leaning on God's act, their bodies at ease.[7]

*

I gazed on my own state. I saw that the parts of my thoughts, my courses of action, and my perceptions are like birds and sparrows and gnats standing up straight before God. It is as if He has placed a chain around the neck of each, or He has tied each of them down with a rope so that they all remain under His control. He Himself bestows upon them life and He bestows upon them taste, so that each of these birds might open up its wings to ease. These birds are standing and looking to see what God will command and over which one He will exercise His control.

I looked again and saw that God was opening up my parts. He showed me a hundred thousand many-colored flowers. Then He opened up the parts of the flowers and showed me a hundred thousand green herbs and flowing waters and blowing winds, and He opened up the winds and showed me a hundred thousand freshnesses.[8]

Remembering God

The reader may have noticed how often Baha Walad uses the name God. In contrast to normal Persian usage, he is employing the Arabic word *allah* rather than Persian *khuda*. He is probably doing so because his meditations and visions are occurring in the context of remembering God's name. Some of the passages of the book make this especially clear, like the following, which is the whole of Chapter 98. It begins as a meditation on the two divine names All-merciful (*rahman*) and Compassionate (*rahim*), both of which are derived from the word *rahma,* mercy. Baha Walad translates the two into Persian as Bestowing (*bakhshayanda*) and Kind (*mihrban*). Then he turns to the formula, "God is greater," and he focuses on the remembrance of the name Allah.

I said, "God is All-merciful, Compassionate." I conceived of God's bestowal in the form of a whiteness and in the shape of an essence compounded of white pearls. I gazed at the essence of bestowal. My spirit came to rest in it and rubbed itself against it. "What a sweet thing is this bestowal, for I have found every ease within it!" I found every release from grief and every healing from pain. I slithered along in it and found no conception of weariness.

I gazed upon compassion and the essence of kindness. I found in it everything to warm the heart, everything sweet, and all loves. The more I slithered into it, the happier I became and the more beloved I found the essence of kindness.

Bestowal is that you have fallen, and a noble, knowledgeable man arrives and prepares your cure. Or, you are broken and hard up. You go to a benefactor and patron and he bestows and provides the cure for your work.

The kind person is he who searches out the helpless and pulls him, willingly or unwillingly, to himself so as to take care of his work. He protects him from affliction and wants to keep him always next to himself. He keeps on adding to the intimacy.

Now I say, "God is greater." If I look at beauty, I say, "God is greater." If I look at any sort of power, I say, "God is greater." If I look at all sorts of knowledge, I say, "God is greater." I keep on entering into the remembrance of God and the meaning of God, for the meaning of God is better than all. The tongue is the key to the heart. The more the tongue moves in uttering the remembrance of God, the more the heart opens up and the more that precious things appear within it. It is as if the remembrance of God is the east wind bringing news of the Beloved. It delights the earth of the dead body by filling it with gardens and orchards. Water flows before the door of every house of the body, and blossoms pour down in the meadow of each organ and part.

An intelligent, experienced man may become sated and tired from the remembrance of God and then wilt. When he sees these wonders, and when that wondrous thing appears to him, his parts become quick and sprightly and they enter into the remembrance of God. It is as if that was a wondrous life that harmed his parts, then brought them to life. Or, it was a wondrous blast of Seraphiel's trumpet that brought the sleeping parts of his earth to life.

The meaning is that this is the explication, by allusion, of how God brings to life the wilted parts and takes them to the paradise of happiness. *By the Mount!* [52:1]. In other words,

when the inward self of Mount Sinai became aware of love, it
fell to pieces. If your inward self also looks cleanly and clearly,
it will become aware and distracted and find that very joy.

Now, utter the remembrance of God so much that you see
God. Just as the veil was lifted from the Mount, so also, when
your veils are torn by the remembrance of God, you will see. [9]

Baha Walad here is referring to the Koranic account of Moses'
request to see God. "And when his Lord disclosed Himself to
the mountain. He made it crumble to dust, and Moses fell down
thunderstruck" (7:143). This verse is the source of the term *self-
disclosure (tajalli)*, which plays an important role in Sufi teachings
about the nature of God's presence in creation. Many Sufis read
it to mean that creation has already crumbled to dust, because
only God is truly real, and his attributes alone are present in the
universe. Like Moses, all of us have fallen down thunderstruck,
because we have no awareness of our own. In truth God is "our
ears with which we hear, our eyes with which we see."

Baha Walad frequently discusses the verse of mutual love. In
the following, he begins by referring to a saying of the Prophet,
"This world is the prison of the believer."

They asked, "The believer is in prison. How can he be happy-
hearted?"

I said: When he is sincere, he will be happy-hearted, just like
Joseph the Sincere in prison. Sometimes a believer does an act
of disobedience and his mouth becomes bitter – "With such a
disobedient act, how can I crave forgiveness from God? How
can I speak to God with need, how can I address Him?" You
must be happy with this bitterness and this brokenness of the
body. You must be content with this apportioning that God
has given – that you are bitter-mouthed in fear of separation
from Him. Unless there is some faith, why would you fear
punishment? If, despite boldness and bravery in sins, you are
happy in remembering paradise and His bounty, generosity,

and forgiveness, that is a faith, a love, and a belief, of whatever sort it may be. In this way, heartache and gladness, brokenness from sins and from bravery in sins, are all proof of your love and proof of your belief in God. Your love for God is proof of God's love for you, for *He loves them, and they love Him.*

Wherever there is weeping and laughing, the laughter is because of union with God's bounties, and the weeping is because of separation from God's bounties. When a human child grows up from littleness, he is happy in God's bounties. In old age, he is sad and weeping because of separation from God's bounties. He laughs in Him and weeps in separation from Him.

Now, if you want your happiness to be everlasting, serve the Everlasting. I mean that if you come to the remembrance of God, the orchard of your parts will blossom, the garden of your soul will begin to laugh, and the east wind of your state will begin to blow. Look and see how God blows with His own blessed breath, bringing your parts to laughter.[10]

If people love the things of this world, this is because God has made the world lovable by filling it with His beauty. But the world in itself is nonexistent, even if it appears to our eyes as a collection of self-existing things. Loving God demands seeing His face in all things without mistaking the gold plating for the gold. One must throw oneself into annihilation, which in fact is the fullness of Being. As Rumi reminds us, "We and our existences are all nonexistences,/but You are absolute Existence, appearing as annihilation."[11] In Chapter 88 Baha Walad explains how God makes nonexistence lovable:

My spirit became busy with my body – "My head hurts" and things like this. It was slithering out from under the body while I looked on. I watched the flowers of intellect and perception, and at every moment the spirit kept banging against the tree. The flowers scattered, and they were stamped underfoot like

ears of grain. Once I came out of the body's skin, no matter
what form came over me, I pulled myself out of it. I was going
into the world of God and howlessness. I was going into God's
attributes. I lifted myself up – "I have been freed from all
suffering."

Suddenly I saw God, standing behind nonexistence and
making nonexistence encompass all things. He was bringing the
things out from nonexistence, and I was seeing the result. I
returned to God's attributes and the traces – the green herbs,
the flowing water, the beautiful houris. I said, "Let me open up
all these sweet, sweet things to each other. I will smash and
throw aside everything that is form and grab the taste of the
unqualified meanings. Such is the reality of the spirit, and such
is God, for He has no howness."

God has made this infinite nonexistence into a beloved. A
hundred thousand beauties, appetites, passions, loves, views,
courses of action, choices, fallings in love, caressings of lovers,
sorts of faculties, kinds of life, stratagems, ruses, embraces,
kisses, sweet meetings – God has pulled all of these over the face
of nonexistence. Someone is needed who can gaze upon
nonexistence, with tears running down his cheeks in his love
for it. Such a nonexistence contains and surrounds my parts
from all six directions. In the end, how will my parts be without
an intimate friend and alone?[12]

Disclosures of God

The experts in Kalam stressed God's transcendence so much that
they often went as far as to deny that human beings can love
God. The Sufis agreed, because God is certainly transcendent,
and a transcendent God cannot be known or loved. But, they
added, He is also immanent. It is the immanent God disclosing
Himself endlessly who is forever the object of love. Love for

anything at all can only be love for Him. This is the theme of Chapter 89. Baha Walad begins by discussing the existence that is truly ascribed to God and metaphorically to His creatures. In the second half, he meditates on the beginning of the Koran's famous "Footstool Verse" – "God, there is no god but He, the Living, the Self-abiding. Slumber seizes Him not, neither sleep. To Him belongs everything that is in the heavens and the earth" (2:255).

> I was thinking – since created things have no congeneity with God, how can they come to be intimate, happy, and at rest with God? God inspired me: "Since the created thing derives from a Giver of existence, which is I, how should I not be its intimate? After all, if existence is not at rest with existence-giving, how does it come into existence? How should the one harm the other? If existence is not at rest with the giving of existence, with what will it be at rest? Since My desire, My act, My attribute, My creating, and My mercy are connected to the creatures, if they are not intimate with Me, with whom will they be intimate? After all, are not all these appetites, loves, and intimacies from Me? Are they not My creation? How should there be no intimacy with Me? Intimacy is My act. All the words between lovers, their whispered secrets, their touching, their intercourse – I bring all this into existence. How can the existent thing not be at ease with the Giver of existence? With whom does it want intimacy to last if not with Me?"
>
> So, utter the remembrance, and be intimate with God and His attributes. Read the Koran and witness the reality of intimacy: *God, there is no god but He.* Since no one's will has any effect but God's, and since I am what is wanted by that will, how should the wanted not have intimacy with the Wanter? *The Living.* Since He lives perpetually, how should He not be intimate with living things? *The Self-abiding.* He makes all your days, and He puts straight all your controlling activities. How

should you have no words and secrets and intimacy with Him? *Slumber seizes Him not, neither sleep.* At no time is He unaware, so how can you not be able to present your state to Him? Let lovers be awake! Are you then the beloved that you should now be sleeping?

Your existence is like a sprig of sweet basil in God's hand – all the blossoms of your appetites and all the leaves of your secrets must be with God![13]

In order for the seekers' leaves and blossoms to be with God, they must remember Him constantly by mentioning His name. The image of God must return to that which casts it, the ray of light must go back to the sun. The path of return is that of awareness and consciousness of the nature of things, of the reality of the world, of the selfhood of the self, of the presence of God in all things and all thoughts. *Dhikr* is an alchemy that transmutes perception and awareness into utter joy. In the following chapter, Baha Walad begins with a Koranic verse. Then he turns to meditating on the two divine names, Life-giver (*muhyi*) and Death-giver (*mumit*), and he suggests how they are connected to the "increase" that the Koran promises in the verse, "God calls to the Abode of Peace, and He guides whomsoever He will to a straight path. For the beautiful-doers will be the most beautiful, and increase" (10:26). Then he reflects on the verse, "Praise belongs to God" (1:2), a formula of remembrance that asserts the presence of God's blessings and bounties in everything good and everything praiseworthy.

I said: God, You have promised – *Nothing is there crawling on the earth but that its provision rests upon God* [11:6]. You have brought me up by way of the manifest doors, so give me my daily bread from Yourself. Since You have not let me do without the secondary causes, I want beauties, I want blessings, I want Audition, I want esteem, I want power, I want will.

God inspired into me: *"God* and *He is God* consist of the happinesses, the objects of desire, and the wills of all creatures. And *increase* – drink from Me without end, like a bee from flowers, so that all your parts may become honey. For We are the Life-giver, and 'life-giving' takes place only through happiness and objects of desire. We are the Death-giver, and 'death-giving' takes place only through separation from happiness and objects of desire. As much as happiness comes, existence appears. As much as happiness goes, annihilation appears.

"All the forms of paradise, like the houris and wide-eyed maidens, pasture on Us. The souls are the drops of Our sweat. The causes of all happiness and all objects of desire are like ladles before Us. As much as you can, drink from Us with the cup of remembering God. Once Our wine makes you drunk and loose, We will give you the sweetness of sleep, like the Seven Sleepers [18:9ff.]. Drink from Us and give thanks for Our intoxication – give news of Our happiness to the creatures that We may give you *increase*."

I said: *Praise belongs to God.* In other words, this eminence is not yet complete for me, since God's exercise of control and God's act are in my parts. He pulled me out of nonexistence and gave me existence. He exercises control over my parts, and I know that He is exercising control over me. This state is the most exalted of states in my eyes, for with this attribute I go to God.

Now I am voicing praise. With each breath I fill myself with this state. I become unaware of creatures and other states. I cut myself off from all familiarity. It is as if I voice praise for the tastes of God, because people voice all these love-letters and all these laudations for the bits of God's tastes. Now, like brides in love I weep: "O God, deprive me not of Your tastes! For I have no one but You. *Leave me not solitary, while You are the best of inheritors"* [21:89].

When anything's companionship with God decreases, the perfection of its state is transformed into imperfection. So also, when a bridegroom turns his face away from a lovely bride, she wilts.

God has a companionship with the intellect, and the taste of the intelligibles derives from that. So also is sense perception. God's exercise of control over me in all my parts, and God's act, do not take place without His attributes, like mercy and generosity. These attributes are all light and leave traces of light in the colors that I see. Streams of light flow in every one of my parts, like molten gold. They flow out from God's attributes.

Since God works in my every part and since all thoughts and all tastes come into being from God, all have turned their faces toward God, who is like a handsome bridegroom sitting among new brides. One nibbles on his back, another kisses his shoulder, and still another rubs herself against him. Or like children – so many pearls, who gather around their young father and play with him. Or like pigeons and sparrows – they come down around him who feeds them and land upon him wherever they can. Just as all the dustmotes of the universe circle round about God's Beauty, so all my courses of action and thoughts circle round about God, uttering glorification and praise.[14]

If "Praise belongs to God" is the formula of asserting God's nearness and similarity, "Glory be to God" is typically taken as the formula of asserting His distance and transcendence. For Baha Walad, it means that nothing is real but the Real, nothing is beautiful but the Beautiful, and joy is found only in God. He sees the same significance in the famous hadith, "God has seventy veils of light and darkness; were He to lift them, the glories of His face would burn away everything that the eyesight of His creatures perceives."[15] Joseph, mentioned at the end of the following passage, is considered the most beautiful of all human beings and the perfect mirror of the divine beauty. Rumi often speaks of him in this sort of context, as when he tells how

love for Joseph so overcame Zulaykha that everything she said
was in fact remembrance of him.[16]

I was saying, *Glory be to Thee*. I said: The meaning of *Glory be
to Thee* is this: If your heart goes to beauty, He is saying,
"Beauty without defect is here." If it goes to property, He is
saying, "Riches without defect is here." If it goes to position,
He is saying, "Position without defect is here." If it goes to
Audition and other people's speech, "Speech without defect is
here." "Mercy and kindness without defect are here." And so
on with all the attributes, down to where He says, "I am the
Guardian [59:23] – A hen does not watch over her chicks like I
keep My friends under My wing."All of this is lest you lose
hope and say, "God is not of my kind. He will not give me
intimacy with the sweetness of His beauty." You will not find
from any kind whatsoever the sweetness that comes from God.

Glory be to Thee. God says, "Whatsoever you love and seek is
not without defect. Since I am pure and without defect, bring
love here!"

"The glories of His face would burn away [. . .]." This is
what the "glories of the face" are all about. I said: O God, the
defect is my own being. My imagination and gaze are the veil
over You while I am seeing You. O God, the shirt of my
existence and senses has been pulled over my head, but the
glories of Your face are beyond the shirt of existence. I want to
strike off the cloak of self-existence that has come over my face
and head, for seeing You is all delight and revelry. To be veiled
from this love and deprived of this gaze are the descending
degrees of hell given sensory shape.

I was shown the attribute of having no defects and the mark
of purity so that I might become quick in love. "Worship" is to
offer love. The goal is to be restless in that Beauty and to
seek It, nothing more. So, O God, when I become weary of
seeking You in the clothing of my existence, which is Your

veil, and when I become slow in seeking, I hold my parts before You like cups – "O God, within these cups bring into being the power and taste of seeking You, for I live through the taste of this seeking. If not for the taste of seeking I would be dead."

Love for the various kinds of beauty, for Audition, and for green herbs is like the morning breeze giving news of Joseph's beauty: "O Jacob, be satisfied with God's Presence in the morning breeze. Come to your own Joseph, and see what will be."[17]

Baha Walad frequently mentions people by name, but most often their identity is unknown. His book is more a diary than a formal disquisition, so he saw no need to explain to readers whom he was referring to. In the following chapter, he mentions two people. The first is Bibi Alawi, a woman who is perhaps his wife, though the sexual appetite she awakes in him sets him thinking how often people are misled by it. The second is Hajji Siddiq. The context hints that he is a pious and Sharia-minded man who has not tasted God's presence in things. The chapter covers a good deal of ground, summarizing the Sufi view of love's transforming power, the difference between formal learning and true knowledge, and the role of the prophets in human existence.

I reached a place where there were ovens for baking bricks. I saw that the inside face was white, the middle was red and bright, and the outside was black. It came to my heart that whatever reaches fire first becomes black, then red, and then it stays white, without changing into another color. The fire of love for God is the same. At first Adam's child is full of heartache and black in face. Then he comes to states and ecstasy, so he is red and brightened. Then he stays bright and white – like the light of Moses, the light of Muhammad, and others among the prophets.

Someone said, "I want to study knowledge." I replied: "Knowledge is of two sorts. One is formal and halfway. The other is the knowledge of the realities. The formal is like theory, rhetoric, and the rules of being a judge and a preacher. All these are cut off halfway down the road. The knowledge of reality is that you look to the end of the work, you strive for that, and you make it flourish. When God gives someone this knowledge and theory, he is chosen, and he enjoys the sweet taste. Whenever this theory is cut off from him, he loses the sweet taste. It is as if the spirits of people like this are unconscious in the World of the Unseen, or they are drunkards, or they imbibe its strength in their own measure. They have other states as well, but *None knows them but God* [6:59]. They become aware of this world only when God makes them aware of it and gives them news of it." I was talking about this when suddenly the dog barked and disturbed me.

Bibi Alawi woke up, and she came to me at the break of dawn. Appetite appeared in me. It came into my heart that this also is God's bringing into movement. Why should it be the cause of punishment and dispersion? God inspired into me: "When I bring into movement, it is by downletting and uplifting.[18] With one movement I exalt, with another I make lowly. Now, when any perception reaches your spirit, first remember God. Remember that God has brought it into movement. Think about it. If this bringing into movement is the cause of punishment, lowliness, and suffering, then ask help from God so that He will not move you like that. If it is the cause of exaltation and good fortune, praise God so that He will keep you in that with every breath. Whenever He gives something of these two states to your spirit, know that you have been chosen for the light of prophecy."

I was standing next to Hajji Siddiq during the prayer, and these perceptions were overcoming my spirit. I was saying: I am amazed that people do not recognize God, since He exercises control over the spirit and these sensory perceptions. These perceptions that wander around the spirits come from God. So, God can be seen as sensory with the eye of the spirit. How can anyone deny God?

Then I was thinking that if everyone had this constitution and this awareness, they would all be prophets. How could this be? The constitution of the prophets has turned away from edibles, clothing, enjoyments, and meat-eating, and their gaze is only upon God. God has given these states to the spirit of the prophets, but He has not given others these states. It is as if God maintains the prophets, one by one, in this constitution. He gives them kingship and makes paradise their empire. As for those who do not have this constitution, who exercise their caprice and appetite, and who find flavor from the foods of this world, when they love the Prophet and follow him, God places them, because of the Prophet's blessing, among the folk of *tawhid* and gnosis and the folk of paradise.[19]

One final chapter can sum up Baha Walad's vision of a universe transfigured by the divine presence. Notice his use of the unusual term "Thou-ness" (*tu'i*). Although the Sufis remember God's name in the third person as if He were absent (*gha'ib*), in fact they are striving to find Him present. The "I" that remembers God meets Him face to face in His name, and, like Baha Walad, it sees the universe as a never-ending array of names voicing God's reality.

When I wake up from sleep, I see the whole world as God's Thou-ness. When I begin to move, I take God's Thou-ness in my embrace to see what will come to hand and what will enter into my senses from it. In the same way, a bridegroom moves, awakens from his sleep, and imagines that he is alone. But when the touch of the bride's locks, the bride's face, and the bride's parts strikes against him, he knows that the bride is with him and that she is his intimate. He rests and begins to speak to her.

I too begin speaking with God's Thou-ness about whatever may be at hand. I enter into the sweet, good, and beautiful things of God. Each instant I mix with God's Thou-ness and gaze upon its nonmanifest wonders. I see its wonders and drink the wine of each one's taste such that I remain senseless until late, just as the sweetest state of Moses was *He disclosed Himself* and *Show me* [*that I may see Thee*] [7:143]. Each moment I embrace God's Thou-ness, for *When My servants ask you about Me, surely I am near* [2:186]. At each moment I have the ardent running of Jesus, the ecstasy of Moses, the undoubtingness of Muḥammad (upon them all be peace!), the unveilings and the stability of the saints, and the beauty of the beloveds along with the state and sweet prosperity of their lovers.

I was given two feet to run to those sweet things of theirs. I gaze upon those wonders and say, "O God, give me of these, for You have brought them into being from the Unseen, and they have come to be like this through Your giving. Give also to me! *Be!, so it comes to be* [16:40], and so that it may also come to be for me. O God, You have given ardent running and happiness to the prophets, the spheres, and the planets. Give me the stability, sleep, and ease of happiness."

The happinesses of the manifest realm take replenishment from the happinesses of the nonmanifest realm, the nonmanifest realm takes replenishment from God's exercise of control, and God's exercise of control takes replenishment from God's attributes. Therefore, the doors to the everlasting garden whose name is "paradise" are God's attributes, and, in each kind of happiness in the world, one door – God's attribute – is opened, so that He may breathe into it and increase it. Now come, let me offer myself to these doors of God's attributes, and let me go into that paradise, so that I may no longer remember the world but remember God and belong to God.

I was remembering God. I said: As long as God does not love me, how can I love God? Love from one side is impossible.

One hand will never clap.[20] In the same way the inclination of the houris of paradise toward its inhabitants is God's love. It is as if God does the embracing, just as, when two forms embrace each other, that is the love of two spirits. But at the level of the spirit's reality and the form's meaning, there can be no embrace.[21]

The fall of Adam

Sufism's rich and diverse theoretical literature deals with every level of Islamic practice and faith. The Sufi theologians recognize the overriding importance of God's presence and nearness, in contrast to the Kalam experts, who insist on God's otherness, incomparability, and transcendence. Much of Western scholarship has dealt with Kalam as if it established the normative positions of Islamic theology, so it is not surprising to see Pope John Paul II write as follows in his book *Crossing the Threshold of Hope*: "[T]he God of the Koran . . . is ultimately a God outside of the world, a God who is *only Majesty, never Emmanuel*, God-with-us" [his emphasis].[1]

In fact, few Muslims would recognize the Pope's depiction of the God of the Koran. The academic discipline of Kalam has had little effect on the way that the vast majority of Muslims have lived and practiced their religion. In contrast, Sufism has affected all levels of Islamic society, not only scholars. As a result, Sufi expressions of Islamic theology have been far more influential in shaping the general Muslim attitude toward God.

The differing stresses of Sufism and Kalam come out not so much in the topics they discuss, but in their language and discourse. The rational methodology of Kalam abstracts God from the world, but the imaginal rhetoric of the Sufis portrays the world as the unveilings of God's merciful face. Reason knows absence, but imagination tastes presence. The Sufis' recourse to imagination explains the popularity of their theological vision in pre-modern times. Abstract categories do not fan the fire of love. Lovers want to be near their beloved. If they cannot have the beloved in their embrace, at least they want to keep the beloved in mind. The mental picture must be beautiful, attractive, and captivating in order to be lovable. It must encourage intimacy and constant remembrance. In short, if God-talk had been left only in the hands of the jurists and the Kalam experts, Muslims would have been stuck with a God who was "only Majesty, never Emmanuel."

Many Sufis read the Koran as a love letter from their Beloved, so they interpret it in the best of lights, even if the Beloved sometimes utters harsh words in His concern to wake up their hearts. A case in point is provided by the Koranic account of Adam's fall. Especially interesting is the interpretation offered by Ahmad Sam'ani, who died in 1140, five years before the birth of Baha Walad and twenty-five years before the birth of Ibn Arabi. Sam'ani reads the story of Adam's fall as proof of God's loving mercy toward human beings. Of course, Muslims in general have never stressed the negative consequences of the fall as much as Christians, and this helps explain why Islam has no concept of original sin. Nonetheless, many authorities saw the fall as the manifestation of God's anger toward Adam, so they highlighted the rupture of equilibrium with the divine Reality that ensued. Sam'ani would never have stressed the positive sides to the fall as much as he does if opinions to the contrary were not common.

Ahmad Sam'ani

Sufi literature is still largely unexplored. Many texts have long been recognized as classics and many others have been brought to light by contemporary scholarship, but still others are lying neglected in manuscript libraries or private collections. The fact that these works are unknown does not mean that they are insignificant. A perfect example is provided by Sam'ani's *Rawh al-arwah fi sharh asma' al-malik al-fattah* ("The Refreshment of the

Spirits: Explaining the Names of the All-Opening King").
Manuscripts of this Persian work of more than six hundred pages
exist in several libraries. A few of the modern scholars of Persian
literature have noticed it, but no one paid much attention until
it was published in 1989.[2] Now that the text is readily available,
anyone can see that it deserves to be counted as a major classic.

Although Sam'ani has remained unfamiliar even to most
scholars, information on his life is not difficult to find. He was a
member of an illustrious family of Shafi'ite scholars from Marv,
and his father was the author of a Koran commentary and a
number of books on Hadith, jurisprudence, and Kalam. His
most famous relative was his nephew Abd al-Karim ibn
Muhammad (d. 1166–67), author of the well-known genealog-
ical work, *al-Ansab*, in which he describes his uncle as an
eloquent preacher, a good debater, and a fine poet – qualities
that are apparent in *Rawh al-arwah*.[3]

Commentaries on the divine names were common in Arabic.
The French scholar Daniel Gimaret describes twenty-three such
works up to Ghazali.[4] But *Rawh al-arwah* seems to be the first
detailed work of its kind in Persian. Sam'ani discusses 101 names
under seventy-four headings. In each case, he begins by explaining the literal meaning of the name or names in question. Then
he lets the inspiration of the moment take his hand. The result
is a series of extraordinary meditations on basic themes of
Sufism.

Rawh al-arwah shows that Sam'ani was a master of all the
religious sciences. But it is the Sufi dimension of Islam that
shines forth most clearly in the form and content of his work.
He frequently quotes Sufi poetry (including verses from his
contemporary Sana'i) and he composes many verses and ghazals
himself. However, his prose is often more poetical than his
poetry, and he must be considered one of the truly great prose
writers of the Persian language. He writes with spontaneity and
joy, while using the techniques of a first-rate stylist. The musical

qualities and the beauty of the text are astonishing. Without doubt he wrote the book to be read aloud. When his nephew tells us that his uncle was an eloquent preacher, one can imagine him reciting passages from this work and producing in his listeners ecstatic states of the type that are often described in the hagiographic literature.

The story of Adam plays a major role in tying together the chapters of the book. Sam'ani insists that every event in Adam's life derived from God's mercy and forgiveness. More specifically, he sees God's mercy toward the human race as reaching its mythic apotheosis at the eating of the forbidden fruit, a *felix culpa* that illustrates the uniqueness of God's love for human beings among all creatures. One could object that he is making sin into a virtue, but this would be to forget that he lived in a society where the incumbency of the Sharia was taken for granted. He is not suggesting that we should sin and be happy about it, but he is certainly asking us to look carefully at our own motivations for activity. Is it correct to follow the Sharia simply because God tells you to, or because you want to avoid punishment, or because you hope to get to paradise? No, says Sam'ani. Human activity must be motivated by love for God, just as God's activity is motivated by love for human beings.

In explaining the significance of the myth, Sam'ani illustrates how Islamic anthropology and psychology are rooted in the divine attributes. A primary goal of the Sufis, after all, is to assume the character traits of God, or to actualize the divine form in which human beings were created. All the discussion of the "stations" that must be traversed on the path to God refer to the character traits that need to be brought out from latency. The models of the perfected divine form are the prophets, and the father of all the prophets is Adam himself. All the perfections, virtuous qualities, and stations that have come to be realized by human beings were already present in Adam. Understanding Adam's story allows us to see how the mutuality of divine and human love brings about the full flowering of human possibility and actualizes God's goal in creating the universe.

The fall in the Koran

When Sam'ani says "Adam," he understands the word to refer to the first or archetypal human being, whose fundamental qualities are shared by all human beings (this usage is already found in the Koran, as in 7:11). He almost never refers explicitly to Eve, not because women are unimportant, but because he is not concerned with those parts of the myth that allow for a differentiation of gender roles. Since he is dealing with the question of what it means to be human, he can ignore the question of what it means to be a man or a woman. Adam's fall is the fall of everyone, and Eve plays no special role. The "fault" of the fall can certainly not be pinned on her alone. If it could be, Sam'ani would no doubt give her a much more elevated position than she already has, because it is the sinning that makes human beings so unique and special.

Sam'ani's views on Adam's fall need to be understood in the context of the Koranic story. Let me summarize the events that he finds especially important:

God decided to place a vicegerent in the earth. Before creating him, He informed the angels about His decision. They objected to God's decision and said, "What, will You place therein one who will do corruption there, and shed blood, while we glorify You in praise and call You holy?" (2:30). God simply replied that He knew something that they did not.

Having created Adam, God taught him all the names, which are the names of the creatures inasmuch as they are signs and traces of God's attributes, or the names of God Himself. God asked the angels the names, but they all admitted their ignorance. God told Adam to teach the angels the names, and He reminded the angels that He had said that He knew something that they did not know. Then God commanded the angels to prostrate themselves before Adam, and they all did so, except Iblis, who is Satan. When God asked Iblis why he refused, he said that he was created of fire, which made him better than Adam, who was created of clay.

According to a hadith. God kneaded Adam's clay for forty days with His own two hands. Clearly, this is a great deal of attention for God to pay to a single creature, since in creating other things, He simply said "Be," and it took Him only six days to create the whole universe. After having kneaded Adam's clay. God blew into him of His own spirit. Perhaps at this point He offered the Trust to the heavens, the earth, and the mountains, but they all refused. The human being – here the term *insan* rather than *adam* is employed – carried the Trust, and, the Koran tells us in concluding the verse, "He was very ignorant, a great wrongdoer" (33:72). Within this same mythic time frame, God took all of Adam's descendants out from his loins and addressed them at the Covenant of Alast.

By this time God had created Eve as Adam's companion and placed them in the Garden to roam freely wherever they wished. However, they were told not to approach "this tree," which the tradition identifies as wheat. When Adam and Eve ate the forbidden fruit, the cry went up, "Adam disobeyed" (20:121). This is the key event, Adam's "sin" if you like, though in keeping with the general Islamic perspective, Sam'ani usually refers to it with the milder term "slip" (*zillat*). Having slipped, Adam and Eve repented, saying in unison to God, "Our Lord, we have wronged ourselves" (7:23). God forgave them, and afterwards, "His Lord chose him" (20:122), which is to say that God made Adam a prophet. In the same way, the Koran tells us that "God elected Adam" (3:33) along with Noah and other prophets. Finally Adam and Eve were told, "Fall down out of it"

(2:38). This is the fall proper, through which Adam and Eve go down to the earth.

Creation

In explaining why God created Adam, Sam'ani keeps in view the two basic categories of divine names – the gentle and merciful as opposed to the severe and wrathful. When Adam was in paradise, he still had not yet fully realized the meanings of all the names that God had taught him. He knew the names of beauty and mercy, but not those of majesty and wrath. In order to gain this understanding, he first had to come down to the earth, the house of God's severity.

> Adam was still a child, so God brought him into the path of caresses. The path of children is one thing, the furnace of heroes something else. Adam was taken into paradise on the shoulders of the great angels of God's kingdom. Paradise was made the cradle for his greatness and the pillow for his leadership, since he still did not have the endurance for the court of severity.[5]

*

> God brought Adam into the garden of gentleness and sat him down on the throne of happiness. He gave him cups of joy, one after another. Then He sent him out, weeping, burning, wailing. Just as God let him taste the cup of gentleness at the beginning, so also He made him taste the draft of pure, unmixed, and uncaused severity in the end.[6]

Since God is infinite, the possible modes in which the knowledge of His names can be realized are also infinite. This means that it is not enough for the first human being to know God's names. Each of his children must also know the names in his or her own unique way. Only then can every potential of the original human disposition come to be actualized. One implication of this is that hell demands human existence in the world. Hell is nothing but a domain that is ruled almost exclusively by the names of wrath and severity, just as paradise is ruled by the names of mercy and gentleness. The fact that God is both All-merciful and Wrathful demands that both paradise and hell exist. Hence, Sam'ani tells us, God addressed Adam as follows when He wanted to explain to him why He had to send him down out of paradise:

> "Within the pot of your existence are shining jewels and jet-black stones. Hidden within the ocean of your makeup are pearls and potsherds. And as for Us, We have two houses: in one We spread out the dining-cloth of good-pleasure, entrusting it to [the angel] Ridwan. In the other We light up the fire of wrath, entrusting it to [the angel] Malik. If We were to let you stay in the Garden, Our attribute of severity would not be satisfied. So, leave this place and go down into the furnace of affliction and the crucible of distance. Then We will bring out into the open the deposits, artifacts, subtleties, and tasks that are concealed in your heart."[7]

God's gentleness and severity are reflected in the two sides to Adam's nature – "spirit" and "clay." Without the severity of clay, Adam would have been an angel, not a human being, and he could never have been God's vicegerent in the earth.

> Had there been only spirit, Adam's days would have been free of stain and his acts would have remained without adulteration. But undefiled acts are not appropriate for this world, and from the beginning he was created for the vicegerency of *this* world.[8]

This last point is important, and Sam'ani often refers to it. The Koran states explicitly that God created Adam because He wanted to place a vicegerent in the *earth*. Adam could not have been the vicegerent if he had remained in paradise.

Adam was not brought from paradise into this world because of his slip. Even if we suppose that he had not slipped, he still would have been brought into this world. The reason for this is that the hand of vicegerency and the carpet of kingship were waiting for the coming of his foot. Ibn Abbas said, "God had taken him out of the Garden before putting him into it."[9]

One of the several virtues of Adam's fall is that it paved the way for his descendants to enter paradise. Sam'ani tells us that God sent Adam out of paradise with the promise that He would bring him back with all his children.

Adam has two existences – the first and the second. The first existence belongs to this world, not to paradise, and the second belongs to paradise.

"O Adam, come out of paradise and go into this world. Lose your crown, belt, and cap in the way of love! Put up with pain and affliction. Then tomorrow, We will bring you back to this precious homeland and this domicile of subsistence, with a hundred thousand robes of gentleness and every sort of honor, as the leader of the witnesses and in the presence of the one-hundred-twenty and some thousand prophets, the possessors of purity and the sources of chosenness. Then the creatures will come to know that, just as We can bring Adam's form out of paradise through the attribute of severity, so also We can bring him back through the attribute of gentleness."

Tomorrow, Adam will go into paradise with his children. A cry will rise up from all the particles of paradise because of the crowding. The angels of the World of Sovereignty will look with wonder and say, "Is this that same man who moved out of paradise a few days ago in poverty and indigence?"

"Adam, bringing you out of paradise was a curtain over this business and a covering over the mysteries, for the loins of your good fortune were the ocean of the one-hundred-twenty and some thousand pearls of prophethood. Suffer a bit of trouble, then in a few days, take the treasure!"[10]

Love

The Hadith of the Hidden Treasure teaches us that God created the universe out of love for human beings. Sam'ani frequently comes back to the idea that the uniqueness of the human situation is rooted in this specific divine attribute. Within the human makeup, it is the "heart" (*dil*) that attracts God's love, not the "clay" (*gil*), which is shared by many other creatures. In one passage, Sam'ani illustrates how the Koran sets up the opposition between Creator and creature in many different ways, constantly asserting the divine greatness and human insignificance. Only in talk of love does the Koran speak of mutuality.

> God gave news of the attribute of His knowledge – *Surely God knows everything* [29:62]. He also gave news of the attribute of our ignorance – *Surely he is very ignorant, a great wrongdoer* [33:72].
>
> He gave news of the attribute of His power – *Surely God is powerful over everything* [2:109]. He also gave news of the attribute of our incapacity – *God strikes a likeness: a servant possessed by his master, having no power over anything* [16:75].
>
> He gave news of the attribute of His exaltation – *Surely the exaltation, all of it, belongs to God* [4:139]. He also gave news of our abasement – *And faces are humbled to the Living, the Self-subsistent* [20:111].
>
> He gave news of the attribute of His incomparability and holiness – *Glory be to your Lord, the Lord of exaltation, above what they describe* [37:180]. He also gave news of the attribute of our taintedness – *Did We not create you of a vile water?* [77:20].
>
> He gave news of the attribute of His subsistence – *There subsists the face of your Lord, Possessor of Majesty and Generous Giving* [55:27]. He also gave news of the attribute of our annihilation – *Everything upon the earth is undergoing annihilation* [55:26].
>
> He gave news of the attribute of His life – *Trust in the Living*

who does not die [25:58]. He also gave news of the attribute of our death – *Surely you are mortal and they are mortal* [39:30].

Since Lordship is His attribute – *Your Lord and the Lord of your fathers, the first* [26:26] – servanthood is our attribute: *I created jinn and mankind only to serve Me* [51:56].

Since unity is His attribute – *Your God is one God* [16:22] – pairedness and association are our attribute: *Of each thing We created a pair* [51:49].

However, when He gave news of love, just as He affirmed love for Himself, so also He affirmed love for us – *He loves them, and they love Him* [5:54].

Here there must be a secret that will increase the refreshment of the lovers' spirits: Knowledge, power, life, holiness, subsistence, and unity are the attribute of His Essence, and His Essence is holy and incomparable. These attributes are suited for Him. Glory be to Him who is disposed to exaltation and suited for it!

When one looks at the human essence, it is tainted and distracted. It is a muddiness, a dark water, a clay. Hence, all those attributes appeared within it. But, the site of love is the heart, and the heart is pure gold, the pearl of the breast's ocean, the ruby of the inmost mystery's mine. The hand of no one else has touched it, and the eye of no one who is not a confidant has fallen upon it. The witnessing of God's majesty has polished it, and the burnisher of the Unseen has placed its seal upon it, making it bright and limpid. Since the heart's work has all of this, the Presence of Exaltation has a love for it. He held the beauty of that love before the hearts of the great ones, and the traces of the lights of unqualified love's beauty appeared in the mirror of their hearts. So, our love abides through His love, not His love through our love.[11]

Love for God answers to all His names. The angels are cut off from love because they cannot taste wrath, severity, and distance, and the beasts are far from love because they cannot experience beauty, gentleness, and nearness. Human beings are woven from both nearness and distance, both gentleness and severity. All the contradictory divine attributes are brought together within them. Only they can truly love God, within whom all opposites coincide. "In the eighteen thousand worlds, no one drank down the cup that holds the covenant of *They love Him* except human beings."[12]

> God created every creature in keeping with the demand of power, but He created Adam and his children in keeping with the demand of love. He created other things in respect of being the Strong, but He created you in respect of being the Friend.[13]

★

> From the Throne down to the earth, no love whatsoever is sold except in the house of human grief and joy. Many sinless and pure angels were in the Court, but only this handful of dust was able to carry the burden of this body-melting, heart-burning verse: [*He loves them, and they love him*].[14]

★

> Before Adam was brought into existence, there was a world full of existent things, creatures, formed things, determined things – but all of it was a tasteless stew. The salt of pain was missing. When that great man walked out from the hiding-place of nonexistence into the spacious desert of existence, the star of love began to shine in the heaven of the breast of Adam's clay. The sun of loverhood began to burn in the sky of his inmost mystery.[15]

Adam disobeyed God at God's instigation, because God knew that without disobedience Adam would not realize the attributes of distance that allow him to become a lover. The essence of love is yearning and heartache.

That Lord who was able to protect Joseph from committing an ugly act could have prevented Adam from tasting of the tree. But since the world has to be full of tumult and affliction, what could be done?

> Those drunken, languishing eyes
>   keep on filling my eyes with blood.
> I'm astonished – how come that moon's eyes
>   have become drunk without drinking wine?
> How can she send arrows into the heart
>   without hand, bow, fist, and thumb?
> Seeking justice for the lovers' hearts
>   all the horizons twist on the hooks of her two tresses.
> She knew that discord had been sown,
>   so she hid herself and sat in the house.
> A whole city was moaning for her –
>   this is not surprising, it often happens.
> Their feet are bound by her irons,
>   they raise their hands because of her.

Adam was brought into paradise, made to slip, then brought out. "Adam, this is not a business that you could have handled yourself. On the day the angels prostrated themselves, you were not alone. On the day of the binding of the Covenant, you were not alone. There was no stipulation that you should be alone in paradise. 'The most evil of men is he who eats alone.' It is not the work of a noble youth to eat all alone. Come into this world, which is the workshop of seeking. The teacher, who is poverty, will write out for you the alphabet of love."[16]

When God offered the Trust to the heavens, the earth, and the mountains, they all refused, since they did not know the secret of love. But Adam thought only about his Beloved. Hence he did not bother to look at his own incapacity, even though the Trust was a heavy burden that was feared by all of creation.

The poor polo-ball in the field! Caught in the bend of the stick, it runs on its own head, sent by the hands and feet of the players. If it reaches this one – a stick. If it reaches that one – a stick. A frail handful of dust was placed in the bend of the polo-stick – the severity of His Exaltation. The ball rushes from the beginning of the field – the beginningless divine will – to the end of the field – the endless divine desire. At the front of the field, a banner is set up: *He shall not be questioned as to what He does, but they shall be questioned* [21:23]. At the back of the field stands a second banner: *He does what He desires* [85:16].

But a bargain was struck with the ball: "You look at the gaze of the sultan, not at the striking of the stick." Those who looked at the striking of the stick fled from the court. *They refused to carry it* [33:72]. Then Adam, with a lion's liver, lifted up that burden. As a matter of course, he reaped the fruit.

After all, they were children of only six days – [*God is He who created the heavens, the earth, and what is between the two] in six days* [32:4]. An infant cannot carry a burden. But Adam was put in the cradle of the Covenant for forty years, and he was given the milk of rulership from the breast of kind favor. "He kneaded Adam's clay in His hand for forty days."

The heaven and the earth saw today's burden [*bar*]. But Adam saw tomorrow's royal court [*bar*]. He said, "If I do not carry this burden, I will not be shown into the court of Majesty tomorrow." Like a man, he jumped at the task, so he became the point of the compass of mysteries. In truth, in truth, the seven heavens and the earth have not smelt a whiff of these words.[17]

Aspiration and discernment

The mark of lovers is high aspiration (*himma*). They strive only for the Beloved. In order to reach Him, they must turn their gaze away from everything in the created universe, even paradise.

> Adam had aspiration in his head. He took and gave through his own aspiration. Whenever human beings reach something, they reach it through aspiration. Otherwise, they would never reach anything through what is found in their own makeup.
>
> When Adam was first brought into existence, he was dressed in the robe of munificence and exaltation and the cape of anointment, and the angels prostrated themselves before him. The name of kingship and vicegerency was recorded in the proclamation of his covenant. The eight paradises were given to him alone. *O Adam, dwell, you and your spouse, in the Garden* [2:35]. "O Adam the chosen, act freely in the House of Subsistence and the Abode of Everlastingness according to your own desire and want. In the life of ease, be ready for the day of the promise."
>
> Adam's unharnessed aspiration placed him like a sultan on the horse of love. He took the arrow of solitude from the quiver of detachment and stretched the bow to its limit. He shot the beautiful peacock of paradise, which was strutting in the garden of the Abode. He knew that this was the path of the detached, the work of those with high aspiration, the court of those brought near to God. Time, space, entities, traces, vestiges, shapes, existent things, and objects of knowledge must be erased completely from in front of you. If any of these clings to your skirt, the name of freedom will not stick to you. As long as the name *free* does not sit on you, you can never be a true servant of God.[18]

Love, then, means to be free of everything in the created world and to choose God. It is to serve God, nothing else. Human beings alone were created such that they can love God in His infinite, all-comprehensive reality, embracing the attributes of both beauty and majesty, gentleness and severity. When they focus on God by realizing *tawhid*, they escape the limitation of possessing certain attributes rather than others. According to Sam'ani, God addresses His creatures like this:

> "O Ridwan, paradise belongs to you! O Malik, hell belongs to you! O cherubim, the Throne belongs to you! O you with the burnt heart, you who carry the seal of My love! You belong to Me, and I belong to you."[19]

★

> "O accursed one, are you proud of fire? You belong to fire, and fire belongs to you. O Korah, are you proud of treasures? You belong to your treasures, and they belong to you. O Pharaoh, are you proud of the Nile? You belong to the Nile, and the Nile belongs to you! O you who declare My unity [*tawhid*], are you proud of Me? You belong to Me, and I belong to you."[20]

If human beings are to aspire to God, they need to be able to differentiate between God and all else. The key to human love and perfection is a discerning heart, one that sees God in the midst of the confusing multiplicity of creation. Adam provides the model for lovers.

> In reality love has taken away the luster of both worlds. In the world of servanthood, paradise and hell have value. But in the world of love, the two are not worth a speck of dust. They gave the eight paradises to Adam the chosen. He sold them for one grain of wheat. He placed the wares of aspiration on the camel of good fortune and came down to the world of heartache.[21]

★

> The root of every business is the discernment of value. The sultan of Adam's aspiration sat on the horse of his majestic state. Then it rode into the Garden to measure its worth. [In jurisprudence] there is a difference of opinion as to whether or not a

person can buy what he has not seen. But all agree that you
cannot judge the value of something without having seen it.

"O Adam, what is entering paradise worth to you?"

He replied, "For someone who fears hell, paradise is worth a
thousand lives. But for someone who fears You, paradise is not
worth a grain." Hence the wisdom in taking Adam to paradise
was to make manifest his aspiration.[22]

What made Adam great was the fact that he carried the burden
of the Trust, which is love for God. Only he knew the secret of
love, for it was the underlying cause of his own existence. He
knew that his love could be nurtured and strengthened only
when he tasted the pain of separation and severity. Hence he ate
the forbidden fruit.

That great man was adorned with auspiciousness, bounty, and
the lights of perfection and beauty, and then he was sent into
paradise. He wandered around, but he found nothing that stuck
to him. He reached the tree that is called the tree of "affliction"
[bala'], but in fact is the tree of "affection" [wala']. He saw it as
a road-worthy steed. He did not hesitate a moment. When he
reached it, he gave it a kick. That nasty kick was called *Adam
disobeyed* [20:121]. He had good sight, and he saw in it the
mystery of a companion for the journey. And the tree also – it
lifted the veil from its face and showed itself to him: "You can't
travel this road without me." . . .

For thousands of years the glorifiers and the unity-declarers
of heaven had been standing straight in the court of Exaltation
on the feet of obedience to the extent of their capacity. When
the peaked cap of the chosen Adam's good fortune appeared,
they lost themselves to that cap. *When We said to the angels,
"Prostrate yourselves before Adam!"* [2:34]. The one who showed
opposition, even though his obedience filled the earth, was cast
into everlasting separation.

Munificence and generosity sent Adam into paradise, where

he was put on the pillow of exaltation. The whole of paradise was put under his command. He looked it over, but he did not see a speck of grief or of love's reality. He said, "Oil and water don't mix."[23]

When Adam saw that paradise had no value, he decided to leave. But God had given it to him as his own domain. The only way to get out quickly was to break God's commandment.

By God the Tremendous! They placed the worth of paradise on Adam's palm. There was no bride more beautiful than paradise among all the existent things – it had such a beautiful face and such a perfect adornment! But the ruling power of Adam's aspiration entered from the world of the Unseen Jealousy. He weighed the worth of paradise with his hand and its value in the scales. Paradise began to shout, "I cannot put up with this brazen man!"

O noble youth! If tomorrow you go to paradise and you look at it from the corner of your heart's eye, in truth, in truth, you will have fallen short of Adam's aspiration. Something that your father sold for one grain of wheat – why would you want to settle down there?[24]

Poverty and need

Human love grows up out of need (*niyaz*). Sam'ani calls need "a fire in the heart, a pain in the breast, and dust on the face."[25] Those who have something have no need for it. God possesses everything in Himself and has no needs. Only those who possess no perfections whatsoever can truly love God, for only they have absolute, unqualified need. To the degree that people find wealth and independence in themselves and see themselves as positive and good, they will be empty of love for God. The secret of Adam's love was that he saw himself as nothing. It is this self-understanding that the Sufis call "poverty," in keeping with the Koranic verse, "O people, you are the poor toward God; and God – He is the Wealthy, the Praiseworthy" (35:15). Sam'ani quotes a great Sufi on the question of poverty and need:

> Sahl ibn Abdullah Tustari said, "I gazed at this path and I set the eye of insight on the realities. I saw no path that takes nearer than need, and no veil thicker than making claims."
>
> Look at the path of Iblis, and you will see nothing but making claims. Then look at the path of Adam, and you will see nothing but need. O Iblis, what do you say? *I am better than he* [7:12]. O Adam, what do you say? *Our Lord, we have wronged ourselves* [7:23].
>
> God brought all the existent things out from the cover of nonexistence into the open plain of His decree, but the plant of need grew only in earth. When this handful of earth was molded, it was molded with the water of need. It had everything, but it had to have need as well, so that it would never cease weeping before God's court.
>
> Adam's makeup was molded of need, and he received the help of need. The angels had to prostrate themselves before him. He was placed on the throne of kingship and vicegerency, and the angels near to God were placed next to him. But his need did not decrease by a single dustmote. He was taken to paradise, and this proclamation was made: *Eat thereof easefully, you two, wherever you desire* [2:35]. "The eight paradises belong to you; wander freely as you wish." But his poverty did not disappear.[26]

Adam's need distinguishes him sharply from all other creatures, who are satisfied with what they have. Adam can never be satisfied, because he needs God, and God is infinite.

> They say that in the Guarded Tablet it is written, "Adam, do not eat the wheat." And in the same place it is written that he

ate it. *Surely the human being was created grasping* [70:19]. The greed of Adam's children goes back to the time of Adam himself. Whoever is not greedy is not a human being. As much as a person eats, he has to have more. If someone eats something and says, "I'm full," he's lying. There is still more room.[27]

Adam's need for God grows up from his recognition of his own nothingness and unreality. This recognition distinguishes him from the angels, who think of themselves as something.

Before Adam, it was the time of the rich and the possessors of capital. As soon as Adam's turn arrived, the sun of poverty and need arose and indigence made its appearance. There was a group of creatures sitting on the treasure of glorification and calling God holy. They were auctioning off their own goods – *We glorify You in praise* [2:30]. But Adam was a poor man who came out from the hut of need and the corner of intimate prayer. He had dressed himself in indigence and he had no capital. Being unprosperous was his means, so in regret he raised up a cry in the court of Exaltation – *Our Lord, we have wronged ourselves* [7:23].

O dervish! From beggars they take rejected coin in place of good cash. They close their eyes to the transaction. But when it comes to the rich, they are thorough and cautious. No doubt, the angels of the Sovereignty had many capital goods, but among these was a certain amount of self-importance. They had written down the notation of "we-ness" on the wares of their own obedient acts. Adam had no capital, but his breast was a mine for the jewel of need and an oyster for the pearl of poverty.

Whenever coin is adulterated, it must be placed in the furnace so that its adulteration will go and it will become pure. Adam had the burn of searching. His breast was the fireplace of love, and nothing in existence had the capacity for one spark of that blaze. "A single breath of the yearners burns up the deeds of men and jinn and extinguishes the fires of all things." When he turned paradise upside down, it was because of the heat of his searching. The wheat was in place, and the whispering of Iblis was a pretext. Searching for the mysteries was his mark.

"O angels of the Sovereignty, O inhabitants of the precincts of Holiness and the gardens of Intimacy! You are all wealthy and possessors of riches, but Adam is a poor man, and he looks upon himself with contempt. Your coin is adulterated, since you turn your attention and gaze on yourselves. Now you must place the coin of your deeds in the furnace of Adam's need. He is the assayer of the Presence – *Prostrate yourselves before Adam*" [2:34].

The first line that poverty drew across the face of Adam's days was this: *He was very ignorant, a great wrongdoer* [33:72]. "Poverty is blackness of face in both worlds."

So, love for that Beauty
is unbelief?

O noble youth! Aloes has a mystery. If you smell it for a thousand years, it will never give off an aroma. It wants fire to show its mystery. Its face is black and its color dark. Its taste is bitter, and it is a kind of wood. It wants a sharp fire to make plain the secret of its heart. There was a fire of searching in Adam's breast, and its sparks looked upon all the acts of worship and obedience and all the capital goods of the angels of the Sovereignty as nothing. *He was very ignorant, a great wrongdoer.* He was an incense that had to be thrown into the fire. From that incense a breeze became manifest. What was it? *He loves them, and they love Him.*

The young man's trials give news of his nobility,
like the fire that gives news of ambergris' worth.

By God, *He loves them* scatters dust on you, but *they love Him* has no dust. *He loves them* says, "Pick them all up." *They love*

Him says, "Let them all go." When you say, *He loves them,* your own shirt collar says, "You've got nothing over me." When you say, *they love Him,* the Throne comes before you saying, "I'm your slave."

They said to a dervish, "Who are you?" He replied, "I'm the sultan. He's my agent."

Stand up, slave, and pour the wine –
  bring the cups for us drinkers.
Outwardly I call you my slave,
  but secretly I'm your slave.[28]

Humility

Adam's need implies that he recognizes his own incapacity and worthlessness. Need is based on humility, which is the recognition of weakness and nothingness in face of the divine Reality. Humility sees all good as coming from God, all evil as coming from self.

Alms are given to the worthy, and we are the worthy. Our "good" is in fact slipping, while evil is our own attribute. Our father Adam was given the cap of election and the crown of being chosen. Then he fell prisoner to a grain of wheat. What then is the state of us children who have been left in the church of this world? When the beginning of the bottle is dregs, what do you think its end will be?[29]

If our wine is all dregs, that is not our loss but our gain. Sam'ani never tires of telling us that it is the sinning and forgetfulness that make the human state so exalted, not the piety and virtue.

This is a strange business. When Adam lifted up the burden of the Trust, the address came, *He was very ignorant, a great wrongdoer.* But when the angels said, *What, will You place therein one who will work corruption there, and shed blood?* [2:30], He sent a fire that burned up thousands of them. True, friends say things about friends, but they are not content to have outsiders look at them with sharp eyes. "I'll backbite my brother, but I won't let anyone else do it."

When God brought Adam into existence He said, *Surely I am creating a mortal of clay* [38:71]. The angels were saying, *What, will You place therein one who will work corruption there?* Iblis was saying, *I am better than he. You created me of fire, and You created him of clay* [7:12]. The Lord of Exaltation replied, *I know what you do not know* [2:30]. "Don't shut the door on the fortunate, lest you damage your spirit's capital! O fire, you have force, but earth has good fortune. How can accidental force stand up to worthy good fortune?"

O dervish, when these words [offering the Trust] came, they came to the folk of Adam. If some luster from these words had shone on the other existent things and if Adam's folk had been deprived of them, that would have been a great loss.

You should know for certain that the grain of wheat that Adam placed in his mouth was the fort of his lifetime. Mortal human nature demands looking, and whoever looks at himself will not be delivered. This is why the great ones write letters to their brothers saying, "May God give you no taste of your self, for if you taste it, you will never be delivered."

That grain of wheat was made into Adam's fortress. Whenever Adam looks at himself, he looks with embarrassment. He comes forward asking forgiveness, not in pride. If someone wants to be a traveler on the path to God, whenever he looks at God's giving success, he must say *Praise belongs to God.* Whenever he looks at his own actions, he must say "*I ask forgiveness from God.*"[30]

Because of his slip, Adam recognizes that his own shortcomings are the dominant reality of his own existence. He is nothing but dirt. Anything else comes from divine providence. Hence, Adam's fall is the source of his self-knowledge, and the fact that he is "very ignorant, a great wrongdoer" is his salvation and glory.

> If a palace does not have a garbage pit next to it, it is incomplete. There must be a garbage pit next to a lofty palace so that all the refuse and filth that gather in the palace can be thrown there. In the same way, whenever God formed a heart by means of the light of purity, He placed this vile self next to it as a dustbin. The black spot of ignorance flies on the same wings as the jewel of purity. There needs to be a bit of corruption so that purity can be built upon it. A straight arrow needs a crooked bow. O heart, you be like a straight arrow! O self, you take the shape of a crooked bow! They take a bit of copper or iron and attach silver to it so that it may receive a seal.
>
> When they put the dress of purity on the heart, they show the heart that black spot of wrongdoing and ignorance so that it will remember itself and know who it is. When a peacock spreads out all its feathers, it gains a different joy from each feather. But as soon as it looks down at its own feet, it becomes embarrassed. That black spot of ignorance is the peacock's foot that always stays with you.[31]

The lesson that people need to learn from all this is that imperfection is part of human nature, that God knows this full well, and that no one should despair of God's mercy. At the same time, they have to learn from the angels and never be proud of their own good works, for seeing oneself as good is to see wrongly, since all good is God's.

> The angels had no slips, neither in the past nor in the future. But there would be a slip on Adam's part in the future, for God said, *Adam disobeyed* [20:121]. However, there is a mystery hidden here, for the angels saw that they were pure, but Adam

saw that he was indigent. The angels were saying, *We call You holy*, that is, we keep our own selves pure for Your sake. Adam said, *Our Lord, we have wronged ourselves.* God showed Adam that the slip of him who sees the slip is better in His eyes than the purity of him who sees the purity. That is why He gave Adam the honor of being the object before whom prostration was made, while He gave the angels the attribute of being the prostrators. Hence no obedient person should be self-satisfied, and no disobedient person should lose hope.[32]

Forgiveness

Human imperfection leads to the perfection of love. Awareness of imperfection keeps people from gazing upon themselves and allows them to turn all their aspiration toward the Beloved. At the same time, imperfection allows God to manifest His perfections. Without sinners, how could He be the Forgiver? God's forgiveness demanded Adam's fall.

The angels were the great ones of the divine presence. Each of them worshiped without any blight while wearing a shirt of sinlessness and an earring of obedience. But as soon as the turn of the earth arrived, they called out from the top of their own purity and began to boast in the bazaar of "me, and no one else." They said, *We glorify You in praise.*

"O angels of the celestial dominion! Although you are obedient, you have no appetite in your selves, nor do you have any darkness in your makeup. If human beings disobey, they have appetite in their selves and darkness in their makeup. Your obedience along with all your force is not worth a dustmote before My majesty and tremendousness. And their disobedience along with all their brokenness and dejection does not diminish the perfection of My realm. You hold fast to your own sinlessness, but they hold fast to My mercy. Through your obedience, you make evident your own sinlessness and greatness, but through their disobedience, they make apparent My bounty and mercy."[33]

In one long passage, Sam'ani cites accounts of several great prophets to show that each of them performed certain blameworthy acts. This is not a sign of their imperfection, but rather of God's mercy, because He wanted to provide human beings with excuses for their weaknesses. He begins with Adam:

> The perfection of divine gentleness caused a mote to fall into the eye of every great person's days so that those who come after will have something to cling to. Adam fell on his head in the Abode of Sinlessness. The Lord of Exaltation had decreed a slip at first so that the house would be a house of sinners. Then, if a weak person should fall on his head, he will not lose hope. He will say, "In the house of subsistence, in the abode of bestowal, in the station of security, and in the place of honor, Adam fell on his head, and the Lord of Exaltation accepted his excuse. In the house of annihilation, in the abode of affliction, and in the world of grief and trouble, it will not be strange if a weak person falls on his head and the Lord of Exaltation does not take him to task, but instead accepts his excuse."
>
> O greatest of the great! Give back some news of this state. [The Prophet] said: "If you did not sin, God would bring a people who do sin, so that He could forgive them. Surely there is no sin too great for God to forgive."
>
> Who am I with God when I sin
>   that He would not forgive me?
> I hope for pardon from Adam's children –
>   how should I not hope for it from my Lord?[34]

For Sam'ani, the whole drama of human existence is played in the context of God's kindness and mercy. God desires to make human beings aware of their own nothingness so that they will put aside claims and open themselves up to His gentleness, love, and forgiveness. People should never forget that the fall from paradise was directed by the divine compassion from behind the scenes.

> "O tree, put up your head next to Adam's throne!
> "O appetite for fruit, enter into Adam's heart!
> "O accursed one, let loose the reins of your whispering!
> "O Eve, you show the way!
> "O Adam, don't eat the fruit, have self-restraint!
> "O self-restraint, don't come near Adam!"
> O God, God, what is all this? "We want to bring Adam down from the throne of indifference to the earth of need. We want to make evident the secret of love."
> "O servant, avoid disobedience and stay away from caprice!
> "O caprice, you take his reins!
> "O world, you display yourself to him!
> "O servant, you show self-restraint!
> "O self-restraint, don't come near him!"
> O God, God, what is all this? "We want to make the servant plead with Us. We want to make apparent Our attribute of forgiveness."[35]

God's reality is mercy and compassion. The existence that He spreads out in the universe is nothing but mercy for all created things. His mercy and love make the Hidden Treasure manifest so that it might be known. When God's own servants, created upon His form, come to know the Treasure, they experience it as sheer good and utter joy. God set up the drama so that His creatures may reap the fruit of existence, awareness, and bliss. Even the angels with their superior knowledge of affairs were not able to see into this mystery.

> The angels said, *What, will You place therein one who will work corruption there, and shed blood?* God did not reply that He was

not doing that. He said, *I know what you do not know*. In other words, "I know that I will forgive them. You know their disobedience, but I know My forgiveness. In your glorification, you make manifest your own activity, but in My forgiveness I make manifest My own bounty and generosity. *I know what you do not know*, which is My love for them and the purity of their belief in loving Me. Although outwardly their good works are barefoot, inwardly their love for Me is pure. *I know what you do not know*, which is My love for them. No matter what they are, I love them.

"Love's affair is truly strange –
   it's thrown to them without a cause.
"You be happy in your sinlessness –
   they've been taken by My mercy.

"Although your felicity lies in your sinlessness, I desire to show mercy to them. You wear the vest of sinlessness, but they are covered with mercy. You are joined with sinlessness in the state of existence, but My mercy is connected to them in eternity without beginning. You show your beauty and act coyly with your own acts of obedient conformity, but they stay in broken-ness and dejection by witnessing themselves."

On the day that He created Adam from earth. His own generosity made mercy incumbent upon Himself. He said, your Lord *has written mercy against Himself* [6:11]. He wrote Adam's slip through the intermediary of others, but He wrote mercy against Himself without intermediary. After all, earth is the capital of incapacity and weakness. What can be shown toward the weak except mercy?

Except those on whom your Lord has mercy, and for that He created them [11:118-19]. Some of the commentators say that this means "for mercy He created them." He created you in order to have mercy on you. In its makeup earth is humble and submissive, and people trample it underfoot and look down upon it. In contrast, in its makeup fire considers itself elevated and great, and it keeps trying to go up.

Water has a certain innate limpidness and a natural humility, but earth does not have that limpidness. However, it does have humility. When Adam was brought into existence, he was brought from earth and water, so the foundation of his work was built on purity and submissiveness. Then this water and earth, which had become *stinking mud* [15:26] and *sticky clay* [37:11], was honored with the attribute of the hand. For God said, *What prevented you from prostrating yourself to him whom I created with My own two hands?* [38:75]. But fire, which considered itself great, was made the object of severity through the attribute of the "foot." [The Prophet said,] "The All-compeller will place His foot in the Fire, and it will say, 'Enough, enough.'" . . .

God honored earth with the attribute of the hand, and then He fastened His own speech to them: *He fastened to them the word of godwariness* [48:26]. But He showed severity to fire through the attribute of the foot.

The attribute of the hand imparts the sense of lifting up, and the attribute of the foot gives the sense of putting down. Earth was put down by its own attribute, but it was lifted up by His attribute. Fire was lifted up by its own attribute, but it was put down by His attribute.

"O earth! O you who are put down by your own attribute and lifted up by My attribute! O fire! O you who are lifted up by your own attribute and put down by My attribute!"

Iblis performed many acts of obedience and worship, but all of them were accidental. His innate attribute was disobedience, for he was created of fire, and fire possesses the attribute of claiming greatness. Claiming greatness is the capital of the disobedient.

Adam slipped, and we disobeyed. But the attribute of disobedience is accidental, and the attribute of obedience original.

After all, we were created from earth, and the attribute of earth is humility and submissiveness. Humility and submissiveness are the capital of the obedient. God looks at the foundation of affairs and the point around which the compass turns. He does not look at exceptions and accidents.

O dervish! On the day when Adam slipped, they beat the drum of good fortune for all human beings. God set down a foundation with Adam at the beginning of the work. He gave him a capital from His own bounty.

The first example of bounty that He gave Adam was that He placed him in paradise without any worthiness and without his asking. And the first example that Adam displayed of his own capital was his slip.

God made a contract with Adam at the beginning of this business. The stipulation of the contract was that whenever someone buys something or sells something, he has to give a taste. Adam gave a taste of his capital when he disobeyed the command and ate the wheat. God gave him a taste of the cup of bounty when He pardoned that slip.

No sin is as great as the first sin. This is especially true when the person was nourished on beneficence and nurtured through blessings. The angels had to prostrate themselves before him – the throne of his good fortune was placed on the shoulders of those brought near to God. He was brought into paradise without any worthiness. God gave him a home in the neighborhood of His own gentleness. Since He pardoned the first slip, this is proof that He will pardon all sins.

After all, we have a thousand times more excuses than Adam had. If the darkness of clay is necessary, we have it. If the weakness of earth is necessary, we have it. If the impurity of *stinking mud* is necessary, we have it. If some confused bites of food are necessary, we have them. If the times should have become dark with injustice and corruption, we have that. If the accursed Iblis has to be sitting in wait for us, we have him. If caprice and appetite have to dominate over us, we have that. At the first slip, Adam was excused without any of these meanings. Since we have all these opacities, why should He not forgive us? In truth, He will forgive us.

O dervish! They robbed the human caravan on the day that Adam slipped. "The caravan is secure once it has been waylaid."

A blind old man was sitting in the hot sun in the Hijaz eating walnuts and dates. Someone asked him, "Why are you eating two foods that are [medicinally] so hot in this terrible heat?"

He replied, "Well, they waylaid my caravan, and everything that I feared has come to pass. Now I'm secure."[36]

Sam'ani's arguments to prove that Adam's sin was the most blessed event of human existence take many forms. In his chapter on the divine name Generous, he runs through several of them, bringing out in particular Satan's role in the drama. The passage is an extended commentary on the verse cited at the beginning, a verse that has caused a good deal of consternation among the Kalam experts and jurists.

O My servants who have been immoderate against yourselves, do not despair of God's mercy – surely God will forgive all sins [39:53]. It has been reported that someone recited this verse before God's Messenger. When the reciter reached the words, surely God will forgive all sins, the Prophet said, "Indeed He will, and He does not care." Then he said, three times, "God curse the alienators," that is, those who make people despair of God's mercy.

It is reported that Moses said, "My God, You desire disobedience from the servants, but You dislike disobedience." God replied, "That is in order to set up My pardon."

Here a good question arises. What if someone asks, "With all the honor and eminence that have been bestowed upon human beings, why has God judged that they must be tested by disobedience?"

This question has several answers. First, you can say that the wisdom in this is that the servant should not become proud, for pride calls down the veil. Do you not see that when Balaam was proud of God's greatest name, he became a dog? *So his likeness is the likeness of a dog* [7:176]. He was the master of the moment and the heart, but through pride he became more impure than a dog.

Another answer: The cleverness, skill, and mastery of the glassmaker appears in broken glass. Your heart is like glass. The stone of disobedience has struck against it and broken it. The Lord of Exaltation, through the fire of repentance, brings it back to wholeness. *Verily I am All-forgiving to him who repents* [20:82]. Even though He said to Moses in the majesty of his state, *Verily I am God* [20:14], He said to us, *Verily I am All-forgiving*.

Another answer is this: God has two storehouses, one full of reward, and the other full of forgiveness and mercy. "If you obey Me, you will receive rewards and generous gifts, but if you disobey Me, you will receive mercy and forgiveness. Thereby My storehouses do not go to waste."

It is also said: He afflicts you with disobedience so the evil eye of Iblis will not fall upon you. Do you not know that when an orchard is beautiful, they hang a donkey's head in it so that no evil eye will reach it?

It is said: He decreed sin for the servant so that it may be a proof of the purity of the Lord.

It is said: He only wanted to spite Iblis – upon whom be curses! It is much easier on the hunter if no prey falls into his trap than if prey falls in, then escapes.

Also: Wherever a possessor of beauty may be, she will not be protected from the gaze of the people. He set it up such that, if you were adorned with the beauty of purity and if you were pure of the rust of disobedience, Satan would turn his gaze full upon you. God threw you into disobedience so that you might be broken and Satan's gaze would not remain looking at you. After that, His mercy will descend to your broken heart, for "I am with those whose hearts are broken."

Another answer: When someone is pure and purified of defects, both friend and enemy fix their eyes upon him, and everyone envies him. The wisdom of afflicting you with disobedience is that everyone will reject you, and you will be singled out for Him. Do you not see what Khidr said when he broke the ship? He said, "The wisdom in making the ship defective was so that the wrongdoing king not fix his eyes upon it" [18:79]. In the same way, Joseph placed the name of thievery on Benjamin, since he wanted to take him away and single him out for himself [12:70]. The Real wanted to single the servant out for Himself, so He decreed slips for him. When he confessed his sin, He said, "If I make him despair, the defect will go back to My generosity, and that is not permitted."

God says, "I will forgive all of them." He said, "I *will* forgive them." He did not say, "I *have* forgiven them" – lest the servant hold back from beseeching, weeping, fear, and hope. The servant must stay between hope and fear, all the time beseeching, weeping, wailing, and supplicating. *Turn to God, all of you!* [24:31]. *Surely God will forgive all sins* [39:53]. "All of you come to Me, because I will buy you all." . . .

O My servants! Which servants? Not "those who have obeyed," not "those who have responded," not "those who have performed the prayer," not "those who have performed the hajj," not "those who struggle," not "those who give alms." Then which ones? *Those who have been immoderate*, those who have passed beyond the limits.

Joseph the Sincere said, *And He was good to me* [12:100]. This is the utmost generosity. The brothers left no cruelty undone. They threw him in the well, they aimed to slay him, they gave him no food, and they beat him a good deal. He was sold as a castoff for a few dirhams. When the Lord of Exaltation delivered him on the day when his parents and brothers were gathered, he said, *And He was good to me when He brought me out of the prison.* He mentioned nothing of the well, nor the prison, nor the selling. He said, *He was good to me.* Then he said, *after Satan had sown dissension between me and my brothers.* He called them "brothers," even after they did what they did. Tomorrow, the books of your sins and the scrolls of your slips will be hung around the neck of that Accursed One. In the story of Adam, what did He say? *So he led the two of them on by delusion* [7:22]. *So Satan made them both slip* [2:36].

Those who have been immoderate. He did not tear the curtain. He did not say, "They committed adultery, they murdered." He mentioned the short of it – *Those who have been immoderate.* They were immoderate. Since He wants to, He forgives. He does not tear the curtain.

He did not say to the Throne, "O My Throne," nor to the Pen, "O My Pen," nor to the Tablet, "O My Tablet," nor to the Garden, "O My Garden," nor to the Fire, "O My Fire." He said to the disobedient, *"O My servants."* That is enough pride for you – *O My servants!*

On the Day of Resurrection, you will say, "My body, my body!" Muhammad will say, "My community, my community!" Paradise will say, "My share, my share!" Hell will say, "My portion, my portion!" The Lord of Exaltation will say, "My servant. My servant!" . . .

"Do not despair of God's mercy. Be careful not to lose hope in My mercy, and do not cease wishing for My pardon. Even if your sins are without limit, your defects without number, and your slips beyond reckoning, it is appropriate that My mercy have no boundary. My pardon no measure, and My generosity no reckoning."

In the midst of all this, Satan struck out at Adam by saying that he was made of clay. "O Accursed One, you see the outer surface, adorned with clay. You do not see the hidden center, adorned with the heart. [*God has made faith lovable to you, and*] *He has made it beautiful within your hearts* [49:7].

"O angels, you have obedience! O messengers, you have messenger-hood! O pious ascetics, you have asceticism! O worshipers, you have worship! O disobedient servants, you have the Lord! Surely you know that the Prophet has said, 'Whoever does ugly deeds or wrongs himself and then asks forgiveness from God will find God. Whoever finds God and sees his own share with Him will not wish for other than God.'"

Noble youth! When God wanted to drape you with a robe of honor, He said *Your Lord*, thereby ascribing Himself to you. When He wanted to free you from chastisement, He ascribed you to Himself, saying, *My servants*.

Look at the Throne to see tremendousness, look at the Footstool to see capaciousness, look at the Tablet to see inscriptions, look at the heavens to see elevation, look at the heart to see knowledge, look at knowledge to see love, and look at love to see the Beloved.

At the beginning of the verse, He says, *O My servants!* At the end of the verse, He says, *Turn unto your Lord* [39:54]. "O you to whom I belong, and O you who belong to Me! *Do not despair!* Do not lose hope in My mercy, for the servant is not without sins, and the Lord is not without mercy" . . .

Moses said, "O God, why do you provide for the stupid and deprive the clever?" He replied, "So that the clever may know that provision depends upon apportioning, not upon cleverness." On the Day of Resurrection, He will forgive the disobedient so that the creatures may know that mercy is a gift, not an earning. It comes through God's solicitude, not through the servant's worship.[37]

One more passage from the "The Refreshment of the Spirits" can serve to summarize Sam'ani's insights into the true nature of the human state:

Dervish, let me tell you a secret. Hearing this secret, the spirit and the world will shout out at being plundered. It is a secret concerning which speech cries out, "It's not my business to tell it." The pen moans, "Love's pounding has already grabbed me – it's not my business to write it." The ink says, "Our black rug can't cover its manifestation in the realities." The field of the blank page says, "Love's polo-ball has no place here." But I will not speak openly – if you do not tighten your heart. The mystery is this:

In the row of chosenness they gave Adam the Chosen a cup of the limpid wine of love. From the distant Pleiades to the end of the earth they set up the cap of his good fortune and the mirror of his greatness. Then they commanded the angels of the Sovereignty to prostrate themselves before him. But his greatness, honor, eminence, good fortune, high level, and chosenness did not appear in their prostration. It appeared in *Adam disobeyed* [20:121]. In certainty and in truth, the top of these words lies beyond the Throne of God's majesty. Why? Because caresses in the time of conformity are no proof of honor. Caresses in the time of opposition are the proof of honor.

The chosen and beautiful Adam sat on the throne of majesty and perfection with the crown of prosperity on his head and the robe of bounty across his breast. The mount of beneficence was at the door, the pillars of his good fortune's seat were higher than the Throne, the umbrella of kingship was opened above his head, and he himself had raised the exalted banner of knowledge in the world. If the angels and the celestial spheres should kiss the ground before him, that is no surprise. What is surprising is that he fell into the pit of that slip. His straight stature, which had been pulled up by *God elected Adam* [3:33], became bent because *Adam disobeyed*. Then from the heaven of eternal gentleness the crown of *Then He chose him* [20:122] took wing. O dervish, if God had not wanted to accept him with all his defects, He would not have created him with all those defects . . .

O dervish! Do not believe that Adam was brought out of paradise for eating some wheat. God wanted to bring him out. He did not break any commandments. God's commandments remained pure of being broken. Tomorrow, God will bring a thousand thousand people who committed great sins into paradise. Should He take Adam out of paradise for one act of disobedience?[38]

10

The paradox of the veil

The fall of Adam is the veil on the face of love. The universe itself is a veil, and so also are all things within it. God's face is hidden behind every veil, just as His beauty infuses every form, every object of love, every desire. If we could see through the veils, we would see that there is no motivating force but mercy and no object of love but God, for "There is nothing real but the Real." All the veils are ladles that pour God's attributes and beauty into our cups. All of them display God's signs in the manner appropriate to their own level of being. They appear to us as the western horizon, but in fact the west is the east.

In the last analysis, "All veils are He." Yet, none are He. This simultaneous identity and difference is the paradox. The veil, the thing, the creature, is not God, yet, at one and the same time, it is God. What is more, there is no way to find God, no way to see God, except in the veil, which will always conceal Him. The true sun will always rise exactly where it has set. God can never be found, yet He is found in everything, because there is nothing that is not His self-disclosure. Jami writes,

> I said to my rose-cheeked lovely, "O you with bud-like mouth,
>   why keep hiding your face, like flirting girls?"
> She laughed and said, "Unlike the beauties of your world,
>   in the curtain I'm seen, but without it I'm hidden."[1]

The paradox of the veil is simply that things are not God, but God is present in the things. For those who see, the veil is the face. The dialectic that infuses Sufi teachings – the affirming and denying, the drunken shouting and sober circumspection, the rending of veils and hanging down more curtains, the voicing of what cannot be voiced – all of this is the face appearing in veils. All of it tells us that the name is nothing but the reality, but the reality stands infinitely beyond the name. To find the reality behind the name we need to speak the name with awareness. To be aware, we must know ourselves and our Lord. Self and Lord are inseparably intertwined, like name and reality, veil and face.

Sufism differentiates itself from other perspectives in Islamic thought by holding that true understanding is the lifting of the veils that obscure the face of the heart. As mentioned, the most general and common term for this sort of understanding is *kashf*, a word that can best be translated as "unveiling." The very word that plays such a central role in Sufi teachings demands the existence of the veils.

The word *kashf* derives from the Koran, where it is used as a verb fourteen times and can best be translated as "remove." Usually God is the subject of the verb, and He removes "harm" (in seven verses), "chastisement" (in four verses), and painful things in general. In the most significant of these passages for the Sufi use of the term, God addresses the soul that has just died: "You were heedless of this – therefore We have *removed* from you your covering, and your sight today is piercing" (50:22). The "covering" (*ghita*) – a term that is taken as one of several synonyms for "veil" (*hi/ab*) – will be lifted at death. Then people will see clearly.

This verse alone is enough to suggest why the quest for voluntary death is one of the basic themes of Sufi literature. The Sufis support this quest not only with Koranic interpretations that pay careful attention to nuances and allusions, but also with the purported hadith, "Die before you die," and the Gospel saying that appears in its Arabic version as "No one will enter the sovereignty of the heavens until he is born twice" (John 3:3).

Voluntary death is also called by several other names, the most common of which is "annihilation," about which a good deal has already been said.

The barrier

To speak of a veil is to speak of a barrier preventing the viewer from seeing what lies beyond it. One of the earliest definitions of veil as a Sufi technical term is provided by Abu Nasr Sarraj (d. 988): "The veil is any barrier that bars the intending seeker from what is intended and sought."[2] What is intended and sought is God, or God's face.

Discussion of the veil is closely tied to discussion of the vision of God. The Kalam experts agreed that God cannot be seen with the external eye in *this* world, though He can be understood to some degree with the rational mind. The Ash'arite theologians added, however, that he can be seen with the bodily eye in the next world, and their rivals, the Mu'tazilite theologians, rejected any vision whatsoever. As a general rule, the more rigorously Muslim thinkers applied rational principles, the more firmly they denied the possibility of seeing God.

As for the Sufis, although they spoke of the vision of God in both this world and the next, most of them agreed with those theologians and philosophers who held that God Himself cannot be seen with the eyes or understood with the rational mind. Nonetheless, they insisted that He can be seen by the unveiled heart, and that this unveiling takes place, as the Koran suggests, at death. Hence, when the Sufis achieve the death and annihilation of the lower self already in this life, they also achieve the vision of God, here and now. This is the general Sufi position, but as soon as we investigate the texts more closely, we realize that the Sufis are presenting us with a much more subtle discussion, and in order to suggest its subtlety, they frequently resort to the paradox of the veil.

Of the eight Koranic references to the word *veil*, two refer to the veil that separates human beings from God. The first of these is often cited by the theologians to prove that God cannot be seen in this world: "It belongs not to any mortal that God should speak to him, except by revelation, or from behind a veil, or that He should send a messenger" (42:51). The second passage, using the past participle of the verb, associates the veil with the vision of God in the next world, and it implies that the people of paradise, in contrast to the people of hell, will see God: "No indeed, but on that day [the people of hell] shall be veiled from their Lord" (83:15).

The most commonly cited saying of the Prophet in this context is that which begins with the words, "God has seventy veils of light and darkness." Another version, considered more reliable by the hadith specialists, begins, "God's veil is light." Both versions continue by saying, "Were He to remove [the veil, or the veils], the glories of His face would burn away everything that the eyesight of His creatures perceives." Again, the verb translated here as "remove" is *kashf* or "unveil," and it is God who removes the veil, not the creature. to a certain point

Especially noteworthy in this hadith is that light is a veil. This is already paradoxical, because light is that which allows us to see. But light can also be bright enough to blind us, and this is manifestly so in the case of God. And light, it needs to be remembered, is a Koranic name of God. As the famous "light verse" tells us, "God is the light of the heavens and the earth" (24:35). This verse can mean that God's light makes itself known through every luminosity that appears in the heavens and the earth, but it also implies that God's light prevents us from seeing God, since the only things we see through God's light are precisely the heavens and the earth, not God Himself. When the Prophet was asked if he had seen God when he journeyed to Him in his ascent (*mi'raj*), he replied, "He is a light. How could I see Him?" Thus, in the earliest texts, along with the idea that a veil is something that prevents the vision of God, we also have the idea that the most basic of veils is the superabundance of God's light.

Given the fact that true "Sufis" are supposed to have experienced the lifting of the veil, references to veils are especially common in the early Sufi sayings and writings. For example, one of the earliest systematic expositions of Sufism is found in the Arabic work *at-Ta'arruf li madhhab ahl at-tasawwuf* ("Making Known the School of the Folk of Sufism") by Abu Bakr Kalabadhi (d. 990). In the introduction, after praising God and the Prophet, the author turns to praising those great Muslims who had followed the Prophet fully, not only by imitating his outward acts, but also by understanding his words and realizing his inner states. Thereby they shared with the Prophet in the unveiling that he was given in answer to his prayer, "O God, show us things as they are." Notice that Kalabadhi is already hinting at the implications of some of the paradoxes of simultaneous veiling and unveiling, negation and affirmation. He writes,

God placed among [the followers of Muhammad] the limpid and the chosen, the noble and the pious. *Unto them the most beautiful already went forth from God beforehand* [21:101]. *He fastened to them the word of godwariness* [48:26], and He turned their souls away from this world. Their struggles were truthful, so they attained the sciences of study. Their deeds were sincere, so He bestowed upon them the sciences of inheritance [from the prophets]. Their secret hearts were limpid, so He ennobled them with truthful perspicacity. Their feet were made firm, their understandings were purified, and their banners shone. They understood from God, they traveled to God, and they turned away from everything other than God. Their lights tore apart the veils, and their secret hearts roamed around the Throne. Their weightiness was great with the Possessor of the

Throne, and they were blind to everything beneath the Throne. They were spiritual bodies, heavenly things in the earth, lordly beings with creation – silent and observing, absent and present, kings in rags. They were outcasts from all the tribes, owners of all the virtues, lights of guidance. Their ears were comprehending, their secret hearts limpid, their attributes hidden. They were chosen, luminous, limpid Sufis.[3]

In an early Persian commentary on this work by Abu Ibrahim Bukhari Mustamli (d. 1042–43), we find an example of a topic that comes up frequently in later texts – classification of veils into different sorts. In explaining the brief reference to veils in the quoted passage – "their lights tore apart the veils" – Mustamli describes the basic veils that need to be lifted before anyone can be a true follower of the Prophet. Notice the importance of "gnosis" (*ma'rifa*) in this passage. This is the self-knowledge that yields knowledge of the Lord.

The veils are four – this world, the self, people, and Satan.

This world is the veil of the next world. Everyone who is at ease with this world has let go of the next world.

People are the veil of obedience. Everyone who busies himself at the feet of people has let go of obedience.

Satan is the veil of religion. Everyone who conforms with Satan has let go of religion.

The self is the veil of the Real. Everyone who goes along with the self's caprice has let go of God. God says, *Have you seen him who has taken his caprice as his god?* [45:23]. Anyone who goes forward in his self's caprice, He says, has made his own caprice his god.

As long as these four veils have not been lifted from the heart, the light of gnosis will not find a way into it.

The meaning may also be that the light of the gnostics' secret heart has passed beyond the veils of the Throne, since today they see in their secret heart exactly what they will see tomorrow face-to-face. If the gnostics were to be kept busy gazing on the veils at the resurrection, they would not be able to bear it. So also, if their hearts were to be kept busy today with other than the Real, they would not be able to bear it and they would scream. It has been recounted from Abu Yazid Bastami that he said, "If in paradise the Real veils me from the vision of Him for the glance of an eye, I will scream and moan so much that the denizens of hell will feel compassion for me."

The sum of all that has been said about the veil is that everything that busies the servant with other than the Real is a veil, and everything that takes the servant to the Real is not a veil. The light of gnosis is the strongest of all lights, and everything that tries to veil the gnostics from the Real is burned away and pushed aside by the light of gnosis. If the light of gnosis did not stay hidden in the secret heart and were to appear, heaven and earth would not be able to bear it.[4]

Another typical discussion of the veil is provided by Hujwiri (d. 1072–73), author of the classic Persian Sufi manual, *Kashf al-mahjub* ("The Unveiling of the Veiled"). Hujwiri explains that there are two basic sorts of veil. The first is essential and cannot be removed, because it is the servant's fundamental inadequacy. The second is accidental and can be lifted. He calls the first "the veil of rust," and the second "the veil of clouding," deriving his terms from the Koran and the Hadith.

The veils are two: The first derives from rust – we seek refuge in God from that! – and it will never be lifted. The second derives from clouding, and it can be lifted quickly.

The explanation of this is as follows: There are some servants whose very "essence" veils the Real, so the Real and the unreal are the same in their view. There are other servants whose "attributes" veil the Real, but their nature and secret heart constantly seek the Real and flee from the unreal.

The veil of essence, which derives from rust, will never be

lifted. Here the meaning of "rust," "seal," and "stamp" is one. God says, *No indeed, but what they were earning has **rusted** upon their hearts* [83:14]. Then He makes manifest the ruling property of this and He says, *Surely those who disbelieve, equal is it to them if you warn them or do not warn them – they will not have faith* [2:6]. Then He explains the cause for this: *God has sealed their hearts and their hearing* [2:7]. He also says, *God has **stamped** their hearts* [16:108].

The veil of attributes, which derives from clouding, may be lifted from time to time. After all, altering a thing's essence would be strange and marvelous, and impossible in the entity itself. But it is permissible for the attribute to be altered from what it is . . .

Junayd says, "Rust is one of the homelands, but cloudiness is one of the passing things." The homeland remains, but the passing thing disappears.

No stone can be changed into a mirror, even if many people come together to polish it, but when [an iron] mirror becomes rusty, it can be made limpid with a file. Darkness is intrinsic to the stone, and brightness is intrinsic to the mirror. The intrinsic remains, but the borrowed attribute has no subsistence.[5]

A Sufi scholar of a slightly later period, Rashid ad-Din Maybudi, who finished his ten-volume Persian commentary on the Koran, *Kashfal-asrar* ("The Unveiling of the Mysteries"), in 1126, describes seven veils that prevent human beings from "seeing the subtleties and finding the realities." These are reason, knowledge, the heart, the self, sense perception, desire, and will.

Reason keeps people occupied with this world and with governing their livelihood, so they stay back from the Real.

Knowledge pulls them into the playing field of vainglory along with their peers, so they stay in the valley of boasting and rivalry.

The heart puts them into the station of courage and stout-heartedness, so they fall into temptation in the arenas of champions by craving for fame in this world, so much so that they have no concern for religion or their religion's victory.

The self is itself the greatest veil and the enemy of the religion. [The Prophet said,] "Your worst enemy is the self that is between your two sides." If you catch it, you will win, but otherwise, you will fall such that you will never rise again.

Here "sense perception" is appetite, "desire" is disobedience, and "will" is lassitude. Appetite and disobedience are the veil of the common people, and lassitude is the veil that keeps the elect of the Presence from the road of the Reality. [Sana'i writes,]

Whatever holds you back from the way –
    let it be unbelief or faith!
Whatever keeps you from the Friend –
    let it be ugly or beautiful![6]

Ghazali, a contemporary of Maybudi, feels it especially important to explain how knowledge becomes a veil on the path to God, even though, as the Prophet said, "The search for knowledge is incumbent on every Muslim." He writes as follows in his Persian work, Kimiya-yi sa'adat ("The Alchemy of Felicity"):

You may have heard that the Sufis say, "Knowledge veils from this path," and you may have denied it. But do not deny these words, for they are true. After all, when you occupy yourself with and immerse yourself in the sensory things and in any sort of knowledge that is gained by way of the sensory things, this is a veil.

The heart is like a pool, and the senses are like five streams by which water enters the pool from the outside. If you want limpid water to rise up from the bottom of the pool, the way to do this is to remove all the water from it, along with the black mud that is the trace of the water. The paths of all the streams must be blocked so that water does not come. The bottom of the pool must be dug out until limpid water rises up from inside the pool. So long as the pool is busy with the water that comes from the outside, water cannot rise up from within. In the same way, the knowledge that comes from within the heart will not be gained until the heart is emptied of everything that has come from the outside.

However, if a person of knowledge should empty himself of the knowledge he has learned and not busy his heart with it, his past knowledge will not be a veil for him. It is possible that the "opening" [of the door to unveiling] will occur for him. In the same way, if he empties the heart of imaginings and sensory objects, the past imaginings will not veil him.

The cause of the veil is that someone will learn the creed of the Sunnis and he will learn the proofs for that as uttered in dialectics and debate. Then he will give his whole heart over to this and believe that there is no knowledge whatsoever beyond it. If something else enters his heart, he will say, "This disagrees with what I have heard, and whatever disagrees with it is false." It is impossible for someone like this ever to know the truth of affairs, for the belief learned by the common people is the mold of truth, not the truth itself. Complete knowledge is for the realities to be unveiled from within the mold, like a kernel from within the shell.[7]

The veil in Niffari and Ibn Arabi

Enough has been said to suggest that Sufi texts commonly discuss the veil as a generic term for the obstructions that block the path to God. But the texts just cited are rather straightforward and do little to clarify the veil's paradoxical nature. In order to understand this, we need to look at Sufi authors who address it directly. I want to consider two of the most remarkable of these. The first is Niffari, who died around 970, making him one of the earliest authors of written works on Sufism. The second is Ibn Arabi, who died almost three hundred years later, in 1240.

Although A. J. Arberry translated two of Niffari's works from Arabic into English in 1935, he has not received nearly as much attention as he deserves, mainly, I think, because of the extreme density and obscurity of what he is saying. He presents most of his writings as direct quotations from God, and God's words are not always easy to understand. Ibn Arabi calls this sort of visionary interview a "mutual waystation" (munazala).[8] In it the servant ascends toward God, and God descends toward the servant. The two meet in a domain somewhere in between, and God addresses the servant. Ibn Arabi tells us that this type of unveiling pertains specifically to the speech of God from behind a veil – as mentioned in the key Koranic verse already cited – "It belongs not to any mortal that God should speak to him, except by revelation, or from behind a veil." He devotes seventy-eight chapters of his monumental futuhat al-makkiyya (about five percent of the text) to elucidating mutual waystations in which God spoke enigmatic words to him – much in the style of the words recorded by Niffari. However, in each instance Ibn Arabi recounts only a single short saying. All of these sayings together would make up no more than one percent of the 250 pages recorded by Niffari. The rest of Ibn Arabi's discussion is taken up by profuse explanations of God's words. This suggests that a good understanding of what Niffari is talking about requires some thought. In what follows, I will quote a few of Niffari's statements about the veil and, where useful, juxtapose them with some of Ibn Arabi's remarks on the same issues.[9]

Both authors address two basic questions: What are veils? How do we overcome them? This is another version of the issue that has occupied us all along: What is the western side of a thing, and how do we get from the west to the east? What is the self, and how do we come to know it? What is God's song, and how can we learn to dance? What is the name, and how do we reach the reality? What is the finger, and how can we find the moon?

To answer the question of what veils are, we need to situate them in relation to God. The preliminary answer is that a veil is anything other than God. We have either God or a veil, either the divine Face or a curtain concealing the Face, either the absolute Reality or one of Its infinite names. In other words, everything that we perceive and all our acts of perception are veils. This includes all our knowledge of God, all the unveilings that God bestows on the seekers, and all the revelations given to the prophets. All these can be nothing but veils, because none of them is God in His very self. In one passage, Niffari makes these points as follows:

> He said to me: Your veil is everything I make manifest, your veil is everything I keep secret, your veil is everything I affirm, your veil is everything I obliterate, and your veil is what I unveil, just as your veil is what I curtain.
>
> He said to me: Your veil is yourself, and it is the veil of veils. If you come out from it, you will come out from the veils, and if you remain veiled by it, the veils will veil you.
>
> He said to me: You will not come out from your veil except through My light. So, My light will pierce the veil, and you will see how it veils and by what it veils.[10]

In this passage Niffari makes three points: First, everything, including unveiling, is a veil. Second, the self is the greatest of veils. Third, God's guidance is the only way to emerge from the veils. Ibn Arabi makes the same points frequently. Let me deal with them one by one. First, everything is a veil. Ibn Arabi writes,

> There is nothing in existence but veils hung down. Acts of perception attach themselves only to veils, which leave traces in the owner of the eye that perceives them.[11]

The veils, in Ibn Arabi's terms, are simply the things – in the broadest sense of this word. God in Himself is no "thing," because He is one and undifferentiated. He is, in the language of Islamic philosophy that Ibn Arabi employs, sheer and absolute Being (*wujud*). To see God as He is in Himself would be to see God exactly as God sees God, and this is impossible for absolutely everything other than God. The distinction between God and the "other" remains forever fixed, because the reality of the thing – that which makes a thing what it is – demands that it be other than God, and, as Ibn Arabi likes to remind us, realities never change. If realities did change, they would not be realities. This is not to deny that, from a certain point of view, there are no such things as "others," but this is another discussion, and we will come to it shortly. For the moment, we need to understand the viewpoint of God's incomparability (*tanzih*), the fact that nothing is God but God. This is the standpoint of the Shahadah's negation – "no god."

The fact that all things are veils can be explained in terms of the philosophical principle that God alone is the Necessary Being, and everything other than God is possible (*mumkin*). "Possibility" is the fact that things stand midway between necessity and impossibility. In themselves, they have no claim on existence. They are nonexistent things that have the potential to exist. They can only come to exist if God gives them existence. No *thing* can escape its own possibility, for its possibility pertains to its very essence. Ibn Arabi refers to this point while providing one of his many commentaries on the saying, "God has seventy veils of light and darkness."

> The dark and luminous veils through which the Real is veiled from the cosmos are only the light and the darkness by which the possible thing becomes qualified in its reality because it is a middle. The possible thing looks only upon itself, so it looks only upon the veil. Were the veils to be lifted from the

possible thing, possibility would be lifted, and the Necessary and the impossible would be lifted through the lifting of possibility. So the veils will remain forever hung down, and nothing else is possible . . . The veils will not be lifted when there is vision [of God]. Hence vision is through the veil, and inescapably so.[12]

The principle that "vision is through the veil" applies not only to the vision of God, but also to seeing self and everything else. In the last analysis, each thing remains forever veiled from all things. Perfect unveiling is strictly a divine attribute. This is because the true home of the realities is God's knowledge, the "storehouses" of all things. No one can know the realities exactly as God knows them. The realities are what Ibn Arabi often calls the "objects of [God's] knowledge" (ma'lumat) or the "fixed entities" (a'yan thabita) – fixed because God's knowledge of them never changes.

If people can never see the realities, they can only see the veils, or the names of the realities. Ibn Arabi often expresses this by saying that people can never see anything but images. The whole universe, in all its temporal and spatial extent, is nothing but an incomprehensibly vast image of God's knowledge, a single infinite veil over the one divine Face. Or, it is the Breath of the All-merciful, within which the infinite words of God become articulated for all eternity. In one of many passages in which he speaks of the universe as woven of images, Ibn Arabi writes,

The forms seen by the eyes and perceived by rational faculties, and the forms imaginalized by the faculty of imagination are all veils, behind which the Real is seen . . . Hence the Real remains forever absent behind the forms that are manifest in existence. The entities of the possible things in their fixed thingness and with all the variations of their states witnessed by the Real also remain absent . . .

The entities of the forms that are manifest in Being – which is identical with the Real – are the properties of the possible entities in respect of the states, variations, changes, and alterations that they have in their fixity. They become manifest in the Real Being Itself. But the Real does not change from what He is in Himself . . . The veils remain forever hung down. They are the entities of these forms . . . All this – praise belongs to God! – is in actual fact imagination, since it is never fixed in a single state. But, [as the Prophet said] "People are asleep" – though the sleeper may recognize everything he sees and the presence in which he sees it – "and when they die, they wake up" from this dream within a dream. They will never cease being sleepers, so they will never cease being dreamers. Hence they will never cease undergoing constant variation within themselves. Nor will that which they perceive with their eyes ever cease its constant variation. The situation has always been such, and it will always be such, in this world and the next.[13]

The second point made by Niffari was that the greatest veil is the self that sees, for it brings all the other veils into existence. When we speak of the vision of God, we are discussing either God's vision of Himself, or the other's vision of God. As long as the "other" – the thing, the self – is part of the discussion, the vision cannot be identical in every respect with God's vision of Himself. Naturally, there are degrees of vision and varying intensities of unveiling – on a scale, according to Ibn Arabi, that is infinite. But the "other" always remains itself, and the other is finite. The finite can never embrace the Infinite in Its infinity, so it can never see the Infinite as the Infinite sees Itself. Ibn Arabi writes,

God has made you identical with His curtain over you. If not for this curtain, you would not seek increase in knowledge of Him. You are spoken to and addressed from behind the curtain of the form from which He speaks to you.

Consider your mortal humanity. You will find it identical with your curtain from behind which He speaks to you. He says, *It belongs not to any mortal that God should speak to him, except by revelation, or from behind a veil* [42:51]. Hence, He may speak to you from you, since you veil yourself from you, and you are His curtain over you.

It is impossible for you to cease being a mortal human being, for you are mortal by your very essence. Even if you become absent from yourself or are annihilated by a state that overtakes you, your mortal humanity will abide in its entity. Hence the curtain is let down, and the eye will never fall upon anything but a curtain, since it falls upon nothing but a form . . . There is no escape from the curtain, for there is no escape from you.[14]

Niffari's third point was that only God's guidance can deliver people from the veils. The seekers can never rend the veils, but God can remove some or many of them. Each time a veil is lifted, the seekers move closer to the object of their quest. The result of the lifting may be inexpressible ecstasy or extraordinary influxes of visionary knowledge, but again, in the last analysis, to emerge from one veil is to enter into another. In the following passage, Ibn Arabi discusses the veils as the "occasions" or the "secondary causes" (*asbab*) through which God establishes the order of the universe.

Since it is God who has established the occasions, He does not lift them for anyone. What He does is to give some of His servants enough of the light of guidance so that they can walk in the darknesses of the occasions. He does nothing else. Then, through that, they see face-to-face in the measure of their own lights.

The veils – which are the occasions – are hung down and will never be lifted, so do not wish for that! If the Real transfers you *from* one occasion, He will only transfer you *to* another occasion. Moreover, He will never let you lose the occasion completely.

After all, the *cord of God* [3:103] to which He commanded you to cling is an occasion, and that is the Sharia. It is the strongest and most truthful occasion. In its hand is the light by which one can be guided *in the darknesses of the land and the sea* [6:97] of these occasions. Whoever does such and such – which is the occasion – will be recompensed with such and such. So, wish not for that which cannot be wished for! Instead, ask God to sprinkle something of that light on your essence.[15]

Ibn Arabi again discusses the divine wisdom that has established the veils in a chapter on "obliteration" (*mahw*), a state achieved on the Sufi path through which all awareness of the individual self is erased by the intensity of the unveiling. He explains that this does not mean that all the veils have been lifted, as some Sufis have claimed. If it did, there would be no acquisition of knowledge, but this is not the case.

When someone achieves obliteration, his *reliance* on the occasions is obliterated, not the occasions themselves. God will never make the wisdom in things ineffectual. The occasions are veils that were established by God and will never be lifted. The greatest of these veils is your own entity. Your own entity is the occasion of the existence of your knowledge of God, since such knowledge cannot exist except in your entity. It is impossible for *you* to be lifted, since God desires for you to know Him. Hence He "obliterates" you from yourself, and then you do not halt with the existence of your own entity and the manifestation of its properties.[16]

In the passage quoted from Niffari, God said to him, "You will not come out from your veil except through My light." This might be read to mean that God's light can bestow full deliverance from the veils. But many other passages suggest that Niffari holds that the lifting of one veil is simply the letting down of another. For example, he writes,

He said to me: Making manifest is My veil, and making manifest has nonmanifest domains that are My veil. The nonmanifest domains have degrees that are My veil. The degrees have ends that are My veil. The ends have furthest limits that are My veil. The furthest limits have attainments that are My veil. The attainments have knowledges that are My veil. The knowledges have sorts that are My veil. The sorts have judgments that are My veil. The judgments have verdicts that are My veil. The verdicts have overturners that are My veil. The overturners have successors that are My veil. Behind the successors is My command, which is My veil.

He said to me: My veils that can be communicated are but a speck of My veils that cannot be communicated.[17]

In short, veils are infinite and inescapable, but the light of God's guidance allows the seeker to grasp what they are and to understand how to put them to good use in achieving deliverance from everything other than God. Niffari writes,

He said to me: If I call you, do not expect the veils to be thrown aside by your following Me, for you cannot reckon their number, and you will never be able to throw them aside.

He said to me: If you were able to throw aside the veils, where would you throw them? Throwing is a veil, and the "where" to which it is thrown is a veil. So follow Me. I will throw aside your veils, and what I throw aside will not return. I will guide you on your path, and what I guide will not go astray.[18]

Only God's light can dispel the darkness brought about by the greatest of veils, which is the self. This darkness can be called "ignorance," and its opposite "knowledge." But, as we have seen, knowledge itself can be a veil and, in the last analysis, it can be nothing but a veil, since it, too, is other than God. Still, we need to distinguish between knowledge that blocks the path to

God and knowledge that assists in traveling the path. As God said to Niffari, "O My servant! A knowledge in which you see Me is the path to Me, and a knowledge in which you do not see Me is the captivating veil."[19] To be a liberating veil, knowledge must see God in and through the veils. Otherwise, most knowledge captivates and imprisons. One must empty oneself of all knowledge, all awareness of self and others, all things, in order to see God. This is true knowledge, the liberating veil. Niffari writes,

> He said to me: I am gazing upon you, and I love for you to gaze upon Me, but all appearance veils you from Me. Your self is your veil, your knowledge is your veil, your gnosis is your veil, your names are your veil, and My making Myself known to you is your veil. So expel from your heart everything, and expel from your heart knowledge of everything and remembrance of everything. Whenever I make something appear to your heart, cast it back to its appearing and empty your heart for Me, so that you may gaze upon Me and not overcome Me.[20]

By guiding people on the path. God does not do away with the veils, since that is impossible. What he does do, in Niffari's terms, is to take people from the "far veil," which is ignorance, or seeing the western face, to the "near veil," which is the recognition of God's radiant light shining through the veils, or the vision of the eastern face of things.

> O My servant! If knowledge does not expel you from knowledge, and if you enter from knowledge only into knowledge, then you are veiled from knowledge.
>
> O My servant! Veil yourself from knowledge by knowledge, and you will be veiled by a near veil. Do not veil yourself from knowledge by ignorance, lest you be veiled by a far veil.
>
> O My servant! Cast your knowledge and your ignorance into the sea. I will take you as a servant and I will inscribe you as secure.[21]

main point

In short, these passages tell us that the veils will never be lifted, but that God's guidance can give people security and safety from the dangers of being veiled. It follows that true knowledge is not really "unveiling." Rather, it is the lifting of the far veils so that they may be replaced by the near veils; or, it is the recognition of the veils for what they are.

The veil as face

This brings us again to the question of the reality of the veils. What exactly are they? Although from one point of view nothing can ever be seen but a veil, from a second, complementary point of view – to which I alluded earlier – every veil is simply another form of God's face. This is the standpoint of seeing the similarity of all things to God (*tashbih*). It is the perspective of the Shahadah's affirmation, the "but God."

According to the Arabic dictionaries the "face" (*wajh*) of a thing can be its reality, essence, and self. God's face is the underlying reality that gives rise to every other reality. Other faces are veils over the divine face, but the divine face has given rise to them, so they are nothing but its manifestations or disclosures. Every reality manifests the divine face. Inasmuch as it is truly a reality, it is truly the face of God. "All are He." Here, then, we have the paradox: God is hidden by exactly what makes Him visible. Ibn Arabi writes,

> He is perpetual Being, and the entities of the possible things become manifest through their properties from behind the veil of His Being because of His subtlety. We see the entities of the possible things – which are our entities – from behind the veil of His Being, but we do not see Him . . . *God is subtle to His servants* [42:19]. Part of His subtlety is that He comes to them in everything in which they are, but the servants' eyes fall only upon

the occasions that they witness, so they ascribe what they are busy with to the occasions. Thus the Real becomes manifest by being veiled, so He is the Manifest/the Veiled . . . No eye witnesses anything other than He, and no veils are lifted from Him.[22]

One side of this paradoxical situation is that seeking to lift the veil is itself the veil. Niffari tells us that God said to him, "O My servant! I have entrusted My veil to your seeking for Me."[23] Or again:

> O my servant! What are you seeking from Me? If you are seeking what you know, then you are satisfied with the veil. But if you are seeking what you do not know, then you are seeking the veil.[24]

Seeking for the face of God rises up from the self, and the self is the veil of veils. True vision of things as they are allows one to see that there is no self, so there is no veil. From the point of view of "All are He," there is only God's disclosure of Himself, so there is nothing but the divine face. This seems to be what Ibn Arabi is getting at in this passage:

> There is no veil and there is no curtain. Nothing hides Him but His manifestation. Were the selves to halt with what has become manifest, they would know the situation as it is in itself. However, they seek something that is absent from them, so their seeking is identical with their veil. Hence *They measured not* what has become manifest *with its true measure* [6:91] because they are busy with what they imagine to be nonmanifest to them.
>
> Nothing is nonmanifest. The lack of knowledge has made it nonmanifest. There is nothing nonmanifest in the case of the Real, for He has addressed us by saying that *He is the Manifest and the Nonmanifest,* and *the First and the Last* [57:3]. In other words, what you seek in the nonmanifest domain is manifest, so do not weary yourself.[25]

People are veiled only because of the lack of knowledge. God has not shown them things as they are. When He does, they will be delivered from the ignorance of thinking that they can know God in Himself, and they will recognize that "Incapacity to perceive is perception." They will see that not knowing is knowledge, and the veil is the face. Niffari often makes this point.

> He said to me: Once you have seen Me, unveiling and the veil will be equal.[26]

*

> He said: You will not stand in vision until you see My veil as vision and My vision as veil.[27]

*

> He said: O My servant! There is a veil that is not unveiled, and an unveiling that is not veiled. The veil that is not unveiled is knowledge of Me, and the unveiling that is not veiled is knowledge of Me.[28]

*

> He made me stand in the veil. Then I saw that He has veiled Himself from a group through Himself and that He has veiled Himself from a group through His creation.
>
> He said to me: No veil remains. Then I saw all eyes gazing at His face, staring. They see Him in everything through which He veils Himself, and when they lower their gaze, they see Him in themselves.
>
> He said to Me: They see Me, and I veil them through their vision of Me from Me.[29]

Ignorance is both veil and unveiling. This is the actual state of all created things forever. People will always remain ignorant of the reality, and they will always know only the name. Yet, the veil is the same as the face, and the name is identical with the reality. The negation is the affirmation. *La ilaha illa Allah*. This is the veil's paradox, and it is also the paradox of Bushanji's description of Sufism. Today Sufism is a name without a reality. Here we are, talking about realities by naming names, and the reality continues to elude us. Yet Sufism used to be a reality without a name, because we used to be in the embrace of the Beloved, drunk with Alast. Bushanji points to the veiling names that block the paths of all seekers, but he also points to the once and future union with the Beloved that is the reality of Sufism.

I close with the words of Hafiz (d. 1389), probably the greatest of all Persian poets. He is traditionally given the title *lisan al-ghayb*, "the Tongue of the Unseen," because he is uniquely adept at naming realities and disclosing mysteries.

> O Lord, who is worthy to hear this subtle secret?
> She's witnessed everywhere, but she's never shown her face.[30]

Notes

Preface

1. The ten essays have all had previous incarnations, but they are thoroughly rewritten and, in effect, new compositions.
2. Jami, *Lawa'ih*, introduction. This book was translated into English in the early part of the twentieth century. See my new translation in Sachiko Murata, *Chinese Gleams of Sufi Light* (Albany, NY: State University of New York (SUNY) Press, 2000).

Chapter 1

1. Ernst, *The Shambhala Guide to Sufism* (Boston: Shambhala, 1997).
2. "The Structure of Religious Thought in Islam" (1948), reprinted in Gibb, *Studies on the Civilization of Islam* (Boston: Beacon Press, 1962), p. 218.
3. For a good selection of these definitions, see J. Nurbakhsh, *Sufism: Meaning, Knowledge, and Unity* (New York: Khaniqahi-Nimatullahi Publications, 1981), pp. 16–41.
4. For a detailed study of the Islamic tradition based on this ancient division into three dimensions, see Sachiko Murata and W. C. Chittick, *The Vision of Islam* (New York: Paragon House, 1994).
5. The Arabic text reads *al-tasdiq bi'l-janan wa'l-qawl bi'l-lisan wa'l-amal bi'l-arkan*.
6. *Mathnawi*, edited by R. A. Nicholson (London: Luzac, 1925–40), vol. VI, verse 1890.
7. "The Structure of Religious Thought," p. 211.
8. Izz ad-Din Kashani (d. 1334–35), *Misbah al-hidayah*, edited by J. Huma'i (Tehran: Chapkhana-yi Majlis, 1325/1946), p. 22.
9. W. C. Chittick, *The Sufi Path of Knowledge: Ibn al-'Arabī's*

Metaphysics of Imagination (Albany, NY: SUNY Press, 1989), p. 393, note 13. Hereafter, this book will be cited as SPK.

10. The "eastern" and "western" faces of things are mentioned by Shabistari in his famous poem *Gulshan-i raz* ("The Rosegarden of Mystery") and discussed in some detail by Lahiji (d. 1506) in his commentary, *Sharh-i Gulshan-i raz*, edited by M. R. B. Khaliqi and Iffat Karbasi (Tehran: Intisharat-i Zuwwar, 1371/1992), pp. 117–18.

11. *Mathnawi* II, 3067–68, 3071, 3073. For a few of Rumi's arguments, see W. C. Chittick, *The Sufi Path of Love: The Spiritual Teachings of Rumi* (Albany, NY: SUNY Press, 1983), pp. 113–18. Hereafter, this work will be cited as SPL.

12. *Mathnawi* I, 772.

13. *Mathnawi* II, 277–8; SPL 96.

14. Rumi, *Fihi ma fihi*, edited by B. Furuzanfar (Tehran: Amir Kabir, 1348/1969), p. 193; SPL 191–2.

Chapter 2

1. *Mathnawi* II, 1022; SPL 20.

2. For a few Sufi criticisms of popular Sufism, see the remarks of Abd al-Wahhab Sha'rani as described in Michael Winter, *Society and Religion in Early Ottoman Egypt: Studies in the Writings of 'Abd al-Wahhdb al-Sha'rānī* (New Brunswick, NJ: Transaction Books, 1982), pp. 102ff.

3. SPK 283.

4. *Mohammedanism* (London: Oxford University Press, 1953), p. 127.

5. For a detailed discussion of the Islamic intellectual tradition in terms of the creative tension between *tanzih* and *tashbih*, see Murata and Chittick, *Vision of Islam*, part 2.

6. For a good case study of this phenomenon, see Mark Woodward, *Islam in Java* (Tucson: University of Arizona Press, 1989), especially pp. 234ff.

7. For a collection of Sufi texts on sobriety and intoxication as well as associated pairs of terms, see J. Nurbakhsh, *Sufism: Fear and Hope, Contraction and Expansion, Gathering and Dispersion, Intoxication and Sobriety, Annihilation and Subsistence* (New York: Khaniqah-i Nimatullahi, 1982).

8. For the manner in which poetry and music are employed in a Sufi context today, see Earl H. Waugh, *The Munshidin of Egypt: Their World and Their Song* (Columbus, SC: University of South Carolina Press, 1989).

9. *Creative Imagination in the Sufism of Ibn 'Arabi* (Princeton, NJ: Princeton University Press, 1969), pp. 70–1.

10. See, for example, J. Berkey, *The Transmission of Knowledge in Medieval Cairo* (Princeton, NJ: Princeton University Press, 1992), especially chapter 3, which makes clear that Sufis and jurists have sometimes been indistinguishable.

Chapter 4

1. *Mishkat al-anwar*, edited and translated by David Buchman as *The Niche of Lights* (Provo, UT: Brigham Young University Press, 1998), pp. 17–18. For more on the unperishing face, see W C. Chittick, *The Self-Disclosure of God: Principles of Ibn al-'Arabi's Cosmology* (Albany, NY: SUNY Press, 1998), pp. 92ff. (hereafter SDG).

2. See W. C. Chittick, *Imaginal Worlds: Ibn al-'Arabi and the Problem of Religious Diversity* (Albany, NY: SUNY Press, 1994), p. 117.

3. *Al-Futuhat al-makkiyya* (reprinted Beirut: Dar Sadir, n.d.), vol. III, p. 412, line 26; for the passage in context, see SDG 134.

Chapter 5

1. See Louis Gardet's entry in *The Encyclopaedia of Islam*, new edition (Leiden: Brill, 1960–), and J. Spencer Trimingham's *The Sufi Orders in Islam* (Oxford: Clarendon Press, 1971), pp. 194–217, both of which deal mainly with techniques. A far more insightful treatment is provided by Annemarie Schimmel, *Mystical Dimensions of Islam* (Chapel Hill, NC: University of North Carolina Press, 1975), pp. 167–78. For a description of various forms of *dhikr* in the context of contemporary Egyptian Sufism, see Michael Gilsenan's *Saint and Sufi in Modern Egypt* (Oxford: Clarendon Press, 1973), pp. 156–87.

2. *Miftah al-falah* (Cairo: Mustafa al-Babi al-Halabi, 1961), p. 31. See the translation of this work by M. Danner, *The Key to Salvation* (Cambridge: Islamic Texts Society, 1994), p. 74.

3. *Miftah*, p. 46; cf. *Key*, p. 96.

4. This is quoted from the Prophet in Shiʻite sources. See Abbas Qummi, *Mafatih al-jinan* (Tehran: Jawidan-i Ilmi, 1962), pp. 179–207. For a representative sampling of the hadiths on *dhikr*, see at-Tabrizi, *Mishkat al-masabih*, translated by James Robson (Lahore: Ashraf, 1963–65), pp. 476–92. Ghazali brings together Koran, hadiths, the sayings of the pious forebears, and views of contemporary theologians and Sufis in his chapter on *dhikr* and *duʼaʼ* in *Ihyaʼ ulum ad-din*, translated by K. Nakamura as *Ghazali on Invocations and Supplications* (Cambridge: Islamic Texts Society, 1990).

5. *Qudsiyya*, edited by Ahmad Tahiri Iraqi (Tehran: Tahuri, 1975), p. 30.

6. For example, Ibn Arabi, *Futuhat* III 248.17, 438.21.

7. *Miftah*, p. 28; *Key*, p. 70.

8. *Mirsad al-ibad*, edited by M. A. Riyahi (Tehran: Bungah-i Tarjama wa Nashr-i Kitab, 1352/1973), p. 269; cf. Razi, *The Path of God's Bondsmen from Origin to Return*, translated by Hamid Algar (Delmar, NY: Caravan, 1982), p. 270.

9. *Futuhat* I 329.2; II 110.21, 224.34.

10. Translated by D. B. Burrell and N. Daher as *Al-Ghazali: The Ninety-Nine Beautiful Names of God* (Cambridge: Islamic Texts Society, 1992).

11. *Miftah*, pp. 35, 37; *Key*, pp. 81, 83.

12. Attar, *Tadhkirat al-awliya*, edited by M. Istiʼlami (Tehran: Zuwwar, 1967), p. 87; cf. A. J. Arberry's abbreviated translation of this work, *Muslim Saints and Mystics* (Chicago: University of Chicago Press, 1966), p. 51. See also Margaret Smith, *Rabiʼa the Mystic and Her Fellow-Saints in Islam* (Cambridge: Cambridge University Press, 1928).

13. Ruzbihan Baqli, *Mashrab al-arwah*, edited by Nazif H. Hoca (Istanbul: Edebiyat Fakiiltesi Matbaasi, 1974), p. 139.

14. *Futuhat* II 245.21.

15. *Al-Risalat al-hadiyat al-murshidiyya*, MS.

16. *Futuhat* II 229.24.

Chapter 6

1. Ascribing the idea to him, however, is problematic. See W. C. Chittick, "Rūmī and *Wahdat al-wujūd*," in *Poetry and Mysticism in Islam: The Heritage of Rūmī*, edited by A. Banani, R. Hovannisian, and G. Sabagh (Cambridge: Cambridge University Press, 1994), pp. 70–111.

2. *Futuhat* II 111.12; cf. II 325.13, translated in W. C. Chittick, "The Divine Roots of Human Love," *Journal of the Muhyiddin Ibn 'Arabi Society* XVII, 1995, pp. 55–78 (p. 57).

3. Rumi, *Kulliyyat-i Shams*, edited by B. Furuzanfar (Tehran: Danishgah, 1336–46/1957–67), vss. 29050–1; for more on this theme, see SPL 194–5.

4. *Kulliyyat* 17361.

5. *Futuhat* II 167.12.

6. *Futuhat* II 329.5; SDG 22.

7. *Fihi ma fihi*, pp. 176–7; SPL 48.

8. *Mathnawi* V 2735–40; SPL 198.

9. *Futuhat* II 114.8; for an English translation of the passage in context, see M. Chodkiewicz et al., *Les Illuminations de La Mecque/ The Meccan Illuminations* (Paris: Sindbad, 1988), p. 97.

10. *Mathnawi* III 4400–1, 14–15; SPL 198–9.

11. *Futuhat* II 113.2.

12. *Futuhat* II 114.14; Chodkiewicz, *Illuminations*, p. 98.

13. *Futuhat* II 331.17.

14. *Kulliyyat*, ghazal no. 442.

15. *Futuhat* II 326.19; cf. SPK 181. On Ibn Arabi's "ontological" reading of the Koranic verse, see SPK 342–3.

16. *Fihi ma fihi*, p. 35; SPL 201.

17. *Mathnawi* VI 971–80; cf. SPL 202–3.

18. *Mathnawi* II 1529–35.

19. *Futuhat* II 113.6.

20. *Mathnawi* V 586–91; SPL 215.

21. *Mathnawi* I 629.

22. *Kulliyyat* 35477; SPL 209.

23. *Futuhat* II 600.32.

24. *Mathnawi* II 3497.

25. *Kulliyyat* 29753.
26. *Kulliyyat*, ghazal no. 1138.
27. *Kulliyyat*, ghazal no. 920.
28. *Kulliyyat*, ghazal no. 244.
29. *Kulliyyat*, ghazal no. 1826.

Chapter 7

1. *Kulliyyat* 13685; SPL 328.
2. Jami, *Lawa'ih*, Gleam 22.
3. *Mathnawi* VI 3172; SPL 43.
4. *Kulliyyat* 9695.
5. *Futuhat* II 34.3; SPK 48–9.
6. *Futuhat* 11 303.13; SPK 44.
7. *Futuhat* I 279.6; SPK 94.
8. *Naqd an-nusus ft shark naqsh al-fusus*, edited by W. C. Chittick (Tehran: Imperial Iranian Academy of Philosophy, 1977), p. 72.
9. *Kulliyyat* 18177–8; SPL 326.
10. *Futuhat* II 281.27; SPK 130.
11. *Futuhat* II 310.21.
12. *Futuhat* II 459.5; there is a reference here to Koran 18:109 and 31:27. For more on the Breath of the All-merciful, see SPK 130ff.
13. *Futuhat* II 366.29; SPK 213.
14. *Futuhat* II 352.14.
15. *Kulliyyat* 5001; SPL 197.
16. Jami, *Diwan*, edited by Hashim Radi (Tehran: Piruz, 1962), p. 301.
17. *Lama'at*, edited by M. Khwajawi (Tehran: Intisharat-i Mawla, 1363/1984), p. 105. See also W. C. Chittick and Peter Lamborn Wilson, *Fakhruddin 'Iraqi: Divine Flashes* (New York: Paulist Press, 1982), p. 108. On "ecstasy" (*wajd*) and its connection to "existence" (*wujud*), see SPK 212–13.
18. Attar, *Tadhkirat al-awliya*, p. 446.
19. *Kulliyyat*, ghazal no. 3067.
20. *Kulliyyat* 24182.
21. *Futuhat* III 393.23; SDG 285.
22. *Mathnawi* I 3279.
23. *Futuhat* II 170.6; SPK 276.

24. *Futuhat* II 124.5.
25. *Futuhat* I 216.12; SPK 276.
26. Buchman, *The Niche of Lights*, p. 31.
27. *Futuhat* II 396.2.
28. *Futuhat* III 398.16; SDG 249.
29. *Mir'at al-arifin ft multamas Zayn al-Abidin*. This work has been given a rather deficient edition and translation by S. H. Askari as *Reflection of the Awakened* (London: Zahra Trust, 1983). The passage here corresponds to pp. 25–7 of Askari's translation. My translation follows a text that I established twenty years ago from twelve good manuscripts found in the Süleymaniye library in Istanbul. Even in this short passage, Askari's text has some significant errors. Among others, he drops the poem by Ibn Arabi.
30. *Kulliyyat* 22561; SPL 78.
31. *Futuhat* II 93.19; SPK 55.
32. *Mathnawi* III 3901–6; SPL 79.
33. *Mathnawi* I 3052–4; SPL 182.
34. *Miftah al-ghayb*, on the margin of al-Fanari's *Miftah al-ins* (Tehran, 1905–06), p. 296; cf. W. C. Chittick, "The Circle of Spiritual Ascent According to al-Qūnawī," *Neoplatonism and Islamic Thought*, edited by P. Morewedge (Albany, NY: SUNY Press, 1992), pp. 179–209; especially pp. 188ff.
35. *I'jaz al-bayan ft tafsir wmm al-Qur'an* (Hyderabad-Deccan: Osmania Oriental Publications Bureau, 1949), p. 300; cf. Chittick, "The Circle of Spiritual Ascent."
36. *Kulliyyat* 31222–3.
37. *Fihi ma fihi*, p. 77; SPL 212.
38. *Kulliyyat* 9778; SPL 159.
39. *Mathnawī* IV 733–4, 36–7, 42; SPL 325–6.
40. *Mirsad al-ibad*, pp. 364–5; cf. Razi, *Path of God's Bondsmen*, pp. 354–5.
41. *Mashrab al-arwah*, pp. 86–7.
42. *Mirsad al-ibad*, p. 365; cf. *Path of God's Bondsmen*, p. 355.
43. *Mathnawi* III 96–8; SPL 327.
44. Attar, *Tadhkirat al-awliya*, p. 153.
45. *Risalat al-quds*, edited by J. Nurbakhsh (Tehran: Khanaqah-i Nima-tullahi, 1972), p. 50.

46. *Ghalatat al-salikin*, printed with *Risalat al-quds*, p. 99.
47. *Mathnawi-yi haft awrang*, edited by M. Mudarris-i Gilani (Tehran: Sa'di, 1958), pp. 24–5.
48. *Kulliyyat* 13681–2.
49. *Diwan*, p. 41.
50. *Kulliyyat*, ghazal no. 1526.
51. *Kulliyyat*, ghazal no. 515; SPL 332–3. *Tan-tan-i tan-tan* is onomatopoeic for the strumming of an instrument. There is a play on words because the word for "body" is *tan*.
52. *Futuhat* II 384.2.
53. *Futuhat* II 384.7.
54. On bewilderment, see SPK passim, and especially SDG 79ff.
55. Ibn Arabi, *Fusus al-hikam*, edited by A. Afifi (Beirut: Dar al-Kitab al-Arabi, 1946), pp. 199–200.
56. *Futuhat* II 280.27.
57. *Lama'at*, pp. 105–6; cf. Chittick and Wilson, *Fakhruddin Iraqi*, pp. 108–9.

Chapter 8

1. *Aspects of Islamic Civilization* (New York: A. S. Barnes, 1964), pp. 227–55. More recently, Fritz Meier has written a detailed historical study of the text: *Bahā'-i Walad: Gründziige seines Lebens und seiner Mystik* (Leiden: Brill, 1989).
2. *The Unveiling of Secrets, Diary of a Sufi Master*, translated by Carl Ernst (Durham, NC: Parvardigar Press, 1997).
3. *Ma'arif*, edited by B. Furuzanfar (Tehran: Majlis, 1333–38/ 1954–59), vol. 1, p. 91.
4. *Ma'arif* 1:131.
5. Cf. SPL 248ff.
6. *Ma'arif* 1:33.
7. *Ma'arif* 1:31–2.
8. *Ma'arif* 1:34.
9. *Ma'arif*, Chapter 98, 1:139–40.
10. *Ma'arif* 1:130.
11. *Mathnawi* I 602.
12. *Ma'arif*, Chapter 88, 1:128.

13. *Ma'arif*, Chapter 89, 1:128–9.

14. *Ma'arif*, Chapter 94, 1:133–5.

15. On the hadith see SPK 401nl9; SDG 155–63.

16. *Mathnawi* VI 4010ff.; SPL 234–6.

17. *Ma'arif*, Chapter 96, 1:137.

18. The two words that Baha Walad employs here are divine attributes, *khafd* and *raf'*. For Rumi's use of the same two attributes to explain the nature of all cosmic movement, see *Mathnawī* VI 1847ff.; SPL 50.

19. *Ma'arif*, Chapter 240, 1:381–2.

20. Compare Rumi's use of the same "koan" in two passages, SPL 209.

21. *Ma'arif*, Chapter 104, 1:147–8.

Chapter 9

1. New York: Knopf, 1994, p. 92.

2. *Rawh al-arwah ft sharh asma' al-malik al-fattah*, edited by Najib Mayil Harawi (Tehran: Shirkat-i Intisharat-i Ilmi wa Farhangi, 1368/1989).

3. *Rawh*, pp. xxvii–xxviii.

4. *Les Noms Divins en Islam* (Paris: Cerf, 1988).

5. *Rawh* 262.

6. *Rawh* 199.

7. *Rawh* 297.

8. *Rawh* 420.

9. *Rawh* 313.

10. *Rawh* 91–2.

11. *Rawh* 519–20.

12. *Rawh* 156.

13. *Rawh* 2.23.

14. *Rawh* 488.

15. *Rawh* 295.

16. *Rawh* 296–7.

17. *Rawh* 186–7.

18. *Rawh* 120.

19. *Rawh* 598.

20. *Rawh* 420.

21. *Rawh* 170.

22. *Rawh* 314.
23. *Rawh* 236–7.
24. *Rawh* 90.
25. *Rawh* 186.
26. *Rawh* 90.
27. *Rawh* 156.
28. *Rawh* 294–5.
29. *Rawh* 261–2.
30. *Rawh* 205–6.
31. *Rawh* 288.
32. *Rawh* 406.
33. *Rawh* 300.
34. *Rawh* 309.
35. *Rawh* 312.
36. *Rawh* 224–6.
37. *Rawh* 367–72.
38. *Rawh* 150–1.

Chapter 10

1. *Lawa'ih*, Gleam 16.
2. *Kitab al-luma'*, edited by R. A. Nicholson (Leiden: Brill, 1914), p. 352.
3. *At-Ta'arruf li-madhhab ahl at-tasawwuf*, edited by A. Mahmud and T. A. Surur (Cairo, 1960), p. 19. The work has been translated into English by A. J. Arberry as *The Doctrine of the Sufis* (Lahore: Ashraf, 1966); his translation of this passage is on p. 2 of his text.
4. Abu Ibrahim Bukhari Mustamli, *Sharh-i ta'arruf* (Lucknow: Nawal Kishore, 1328/1910), vol. 1, pp. 26–7.
5. Hujwiri, *Kashfal-mahjub*, edited by V. Zhukovsky (Tehran: Amir Kabir, 1336/1957), p. 5. The book was translated by R. A. Nicholson as *The Kashf al-Mahjub: The Oldest Persian Treatise on Sufiism* (London: Luzac, 1911).
6. Maybudi, *Kashf al-asrar wa uddat al-abrar*, edited by A. A. Hikmat (Tehran: Danishgah, 1331–39/1952–60), vol. 6, p. 440. Maybudi quotes the poem from Sana'i, *Diwan*, edited by Mudarris Radawi (Tehran: Ibn Sina, 1329/1950), p. 51.

7. *Kimiya-yi sa'adat*, edited by H. Khadiw-jam (Tehran: Jibi, 1354/1975), pp. 36–7. For a detailed discussion of the veils hadith by Ghazali, see Buchman, *The Niche of Lights*.

8. For a brief discussion of these, see SPK 278–9; for more details, SDG 112–20.

9. For a detailed discussion of Ibn Arabi's teachings on veils and the divine face, see SDG, chapters 3–4.

10. Paul Nwyia, *Trois oeuvres inédites de mystiques Musulmans* (Beirut: Dar al-Machreq, 1973), p. 306.

11. *Futuhat* III 214.25. For the passage in context, see SDG 110–11.

12. *Futuhat* III 276.18; SDG 156.

13. *Futuhat* IV 19.5, 34; for more context, see SPK 231. For the cosmos as imagination, see SPK, especially chapters 7–8; SDG, especially chapters 2 and 10; and Chittick, *Imaginal Worlds*, especially chapters 1 and 9.

14. *Futuhat* II 554.4, 21; see SDG 109.

15. *Futuhat* III 249.22; SPK 179.

16. *Futuhat* II 553.5; SPK 176.

17. Nwyia, *Trois Oeuvres*, pp. 240–1.

18. *Mawaqif*, staying 18, lines 8–9, text in A. J. Arberry (editor and translator), *The Mawdqif and Mukhatabat of Muḥammad ibn 'Abdi 'l-Jabbār al-Niffarī* (Cambridge: Cambridge University Press, 1935). All following references to the *Mawaqif* and *Mukhatabat* are from this edition.

19. *Mukhātabāt* 47:1.

20. *Mawaqif* 14:14.

21. *Mukhatabat* 16:2–4.

22. *Futuhat* III 547.8; SDG 129.

23. *Mukhatabat* 28:9.

24. *Mukhatabat* 33:3.

25. *Futuhat* IV 407.22; SDG 104.

26. *Mawaqif* 31:1–3.

27. *Mawaqif* 55–30.

28. *Mukhatabat* 14:9.

29. *Mawaqif* 47:1–2.

30. *Diwan*, edited by M. Qazwini and Q. Ghani (Tehran: Zuwwar, 1320/ 1941), p. 352.

Suggested reading

General

Andrae, T, *In the Garden of Myrtles: Studies in Early Islamic Mysticism*, Albany, NY: SUNY Press, 1987

Awn, P., *Satan's Tragedy and Redemption: Iblis in Sufi Psychology*, Leiden: Brill, 1983

Baldick, J., *Mystical Islam: An Introduction to Sufism*, New York: New York University Press, 1989

Ernst, Carl, *The Shambhala Guide to Sufism*, Boston: Shambhala, 1997

Izutsu, T., *Creation and the Timeless Order of Things*, Ashland, OR: White Cloud Press, 1994

Lewisohn, Leonard (ed.). *The Heritage of Sufism*, 3 vols., Oxford: Oneworld, 1999

Murata, Sachiko, *Chinese Gleams of Sufi Light: Wang Tai-yil's "Great Learning of the Pure and Real" and Liu Chih's "Displaying the Concealment of the Real Realm"*, Albany, NY: SUNY Press, 2000

—— *The Tao of Islam: A Sourcebook on Gender Relationships in Islamic Thought*, Albany, NY: SUNY Press, 1992

Murata, Sachiko and Chittick, William C., *The Vision of Islam*, New York: Paragon House, 1994

Nasr, Seyyed Hossein (ed.), *Islamic Spirituality, 1* vols., New York: Crossroad, 1987–90

Padwick, Constance E., *Muslim Devotions: A Study of Prayer-Manuals in Common Use*, 1961; reprinted Oxford: Oneworld, 1996

Renard, J., *Seven Doors to Islam: Spirituality and the Religious Life of Muslims*, Berkeley: University of California Press, 1996

Schimmel, A., *Mystical Dimensions of Islam*, Chapel Hill: University of North Carolina Press, 1975

Trimingham, J. Spencer, *The Sufi Orders in Islam*, Oxford: Clarendon Press, 1971

Valiuddin, Mir, *Contemplative Disciplines in Sufism*, London: East-West, 1980

Studies of individual Sufis

Addas, Claude, *Quest for the Red Sulphur: The Life of Ibn 'Arabī*, Cambridge: Islamic Texts Society, 1993

Chittick, William C. *The Sufi Path of Love: The Spiritual Teachings of Rumi*, Albany, NY: SUNY Press, 1983

Chodkiewicz, M., *An Ocean Without Shore: Ibn Arabi, the Book and the Law*, Albany, NY: SUNY Press, 1993

Corbin, H., *Creative Imagination in the Sufism of Ibn 'Arabi*, Princeton, NJ: Princeton University Press, 1969

Cornell, Vincent, *The Way of Abu Madyan*, Cambridge: Islamic Texts Society, 1996

Ernst, Carl, *Ruzbihan Baqli: Mysticism and the Rhetoric of Sainthood in Persian Sufism*, Richmond, Surrey: Curzon Press, 1994

Izutsu, T, *Sufism and Taoism*, Berkeley: University of California Press, 1984 (on Ibn Arabi) Lewisohn, L., *Beyond Faith and Infidelity: The Sufi Poetry and Teachings of Mahmud Shabistari*, Richmond, Surrey: Curzon Press, 1995

Lings, M., *A Sufi Saint of the Twentieth Century*, Berkeley: University of California Press, 1971

Massignon, L., *The Passion of al-Hallāj: Mystic and Martyr of Islam*, 4 vols., Princeton, NJ: Princeton University Press, 1982

Ridgeon, Lloyd, *'Azīz Nasafī*, Richmond, Surrey: Curzon Press, 1998

Schimmel, A., *The Triumphal Sun: A Study of the Works of Jalāloddīn Rūmī*, London: East-West, 1978

Translations

Early Islamic Mysticism: Sufi, Qur'an, Mi'raj, Poetic and Theological Writings (Michael Sells), New York: Paulist Press, 1996

Abd al-Qadir Jaza'iri, *The Spiritual Writings of Amir Abd al-Kader* (Michel Chodkiewicz), Albany, NY: SUNY Press, 1995

Ali ibn al-Husayn, *The Psalms of Islam* (William C. Chittick), London: Muhammadi Trust, 1988

Ansari, Khwaja Abdullah, *Intimate Conversations* (Wheeler Thackston), New York: Paulist Press, 1978

Attar, *Conference of the Birds* (Afkham Darbandi and Dick Davis), London: Penguin, 1984

—— *Muslim Saints and Mystics* (A. J. Arberry), Chicago: University of Chicago Press, 1966

Darqawi, *Letters of a Sufi Master* (Titus Burckhardt), London: Perennial, 1961

Ghazali, Abu Hamid. *The Niche of Lights* (David Buchman), Provo, UT: Brigham Young University Press, 1998

—— *On Disciplining the Soul and on Breaking the Two Desires* (T. J. Winter), Cambridge; Islamic Texts Society, 1995

—— *Freedom and Fulfillment: An Annotated Translation of al-Ghazali's al-Munqidh min al-Dalal and other Relevant Works of al-Ghazali* (R. J. McCarthy) Boston: Twayne, 1980

Ghazali, Ahmad, *Sawānih: Inspirations from the World of Pure Spirits* (N. Pourjavady), London: KPI, 1986

Ibn Abbad ar-Rundi, *Letters on the Sufi Path* (John Renard), New York: Paulist Press, 1986

Ibn Arabi, *Bezels of Wisdom* (R. W. J. Austin), New York: Paulist Press, 1980

—— *Sufis of Andalusia* (R. W. J. Austin), London: George Alien & Unwin, 1971

Ibn Ata'illah, *The Book of Wisdom* (Victor Danner), New York: Paulist Press, 1978

Ibn-i Munawwar, *Secrets of God's Mystical Oneness: Asrar al-Towhid* (John O'Kane), Costa Mesa, CA: Mazda, 1992

Iraqi, *Fakhruddin 'Iraqi: Divine Flashes* (William C. Chittick and Peter Lamborn Wilson), New York: Paulist Press, 1982

Jilani, *The Sublime Revelation* (Muhtar Holland), Fort Lauderdale, FL: Al-Baz, 1993

Maneri, Sharafuddin, *The Hundred Letters* (Paul Jackson), New York: Paulist Press, 1980

Nasir ad-Din, *Faith and Practice of Islam: Three Thirteenth Century Sufi Texts* (William C. Chittick), Albany, NY: SUNY Press, 1992

Nizam ad-Din Awliya, *Morals for the Heart* (Bruce Lawrence), New York: Paulist Press, 1992

Qushayri, *Principles of Sufism* (Barbara von Schlegell), Berkeley: Mizan Press, 1992

Razi, *The Path of God's Bondsmen from Origin to Return* (Hamid Algar), Delmar, NY: Caravan, 1982

Rumi, *Discourses* (A. J. Arberry), London: John Murray, 1961

—— *The Mathnawī* (R. A. Nicholson), 3 vols., London: Luzac, 1926–34

—— *Mystical Poems of Rūmī* (A. J. Arberry), 2 vols., Chicago: Chicago University Press, 1968; Boulder, CO: Westview, 1979

Ruzbihan Baqli, *The Unveiling of Secrets, Diary of a Sufi Master* (Carl Ernst), Durham, NC: Parvardigar Press, 1997

Shadhili, *Mystical Teachings of al-Shadhili* (Elmer Douglas) Albany, NY: SUNY Press, 1993

Suhrawardi, Abu'n-Najib, *A Sufi Rule for Novices* (M. Milson), Cambridge, MA: Harvard University Press, 1975

Suhrawardi, Shihab ad-Din, *The Mystical and Visionary Treatises* (W. Thackston), London: Octagon, 1982

Sulami, *The Book of Sufi Chivalry* (Tosun Bayrak), New York: Inner Traditions, 1983

Tirmidhi, *The Concept of Sainthood in Early Islamic Mysticism*

(Berndt Radtke and John O'Kane), Richmond, Surrey: Curzon Press, 1996

Books by contemporary Sufi teachers

Bawa Muhaiyadden, M. R., *Golden Words of A Sufi Sheikh*, Philadelphia: Fellowship Press, 1982

Burckhardt, T., *An Introduction to Sufi Doctrine*, Lahore: Ashraf, 1959

Friedlander, S., *When you Hear Hoofbeats, Think of a Zebra*, New York: Harper & Row, 1987

Guénon, R., *The Crisis of the Modern World*, London: Luzac, 1962

Haeri, Shaikh Fadlallah, *Beginning's End*, London: KPI, 1987

Helminski, K., *Living Presence: A Sufi Way to Mindfulness and the Essential Self*, Los Angeles: J. P. Tarcher, 1992

Kabbani, M. H., *The Naqshbandi Sufi Way: History and Guidebook of the Saints of the Golden Chain*, Chicago: Kazi Publications, 1995

Lings, M., *What is Sufism?*, Berkeley: University of California Press, 1975

Nasr, S. H., *Sufi Essays*, London: George Alien & Unwin, 1972

Nazim al-Qubrusi, Sheikh, *Mercy Oceans*, several vols., Konya, Turkey: Sebat Press

Nurbakhsh, Javad, *Sufi Symbolism*, 8 vols., London: Khaniqahi Nimatullahi, 1984–94

Ozak, Muzaffer, *The Unveiling of Love*, New York: Inner Traditions, 1982

Rauf, Feisal Abdul, *Islam: A Search for Meaning*, Costa Mesa, CA: Mazda, 1996

Schuon, F., *Understanding Islam*, London: Alien & Unwin, 1963

Siraj ed-Din, Abu Bakr, *The Book of Certainty*, London: Ryder, 1952

Stoddart, W., *Sufism: The Mystical Doctrines and Methods of Islam*, Wellingborough: Thorsons, 1976

Index of names and terms

Index of hadiths and sayings

Index of Koranic verses